"I don't know about you, but I [...] doing war with my longing for [...] losing. One huge part of the problem is that we're not having conversations about how the gospel is the balm for our desire to keep it all together. No one is talking about how God's Word is the lamp our feet so desperately need because we're fumbling and falling over our own self-sufficiency. Instead, we're praised when playing with the idol of control. Enter Sharon. She is our wise pal, our gentle and knowledgeable pastor friend. With care, curiosity, and boldness she's leading us to lay down control in a kingdom way. I am so grateful. Please read this book."

Jess Connolly, author of *Breaking Free from Body Shame* and *You Are the Girl for the Job*

"In *The Cost of Control* Sharon is at her best. Her theologically rich words are wise, helpful, and transformative. Discover the freedom you were created for."

Dr. Derwin L. Gray, cofounder of Transformation Church and author of *How to Heal Our Racial Divide*

"We live in an anxious culture, and at the core of it is our need to be in control. Even more, society disciples us into an anxiety-ridden life, forming us to believe that more control is the solution. With sharp theological and psychological understanding, Sharon shows us how faulty this thinking is and opens a world of insight that we desperately need to loosen the grip—or rather be freed from the grip—of the illusion of control. This book is a gift."

Rich Villodas, pastor of New Life Fellowship and author of *The Deeply Formed Life*

"Sharon Hodde Miller is a voice every leader needs to be listening to. Sharon's mix of confession, theological insight, and observations about the human condition in *The Cost of Control* are convicting, helpful, and liberating."

Carey Nieuwhof, speaker, podcaster, and bestselling author of *At Your Best*

"I am more and more convinced that self-awareness is a good start on the road to freedom, but what we really need is a trusted guide offering us a path. In *The Cost of Control* Sharon Hodde Miller skillfully takes a deep dive into control—why we want it, how we wield it, and how it gets hold of us. With plenty of study, keen observation, and confession, Sharon offers us a way to explore our own control dynamics so we can be freed from their grip. I appreciate how Sharon first shows us what control offers us (which is why we want it) before showing us the cost of it and ultimately how we can yield it to God. *The Cost of Control* is timely and essential for thriving nowadays."

Steve Cuss, pastor and author of
Managing Leadership Anxiety

"You might not think of yourself as a person who struggles with control. Think again. In this illuminating book, Sharon Hodde Miller offers a thoughtful, well-researched guide on the oldest sin of humankind and how that sin infects all of us. Her clarion call to name our control issues—and then to unravel ourselves from them—couldn't come at a better time for our culture. Sharon is a respected truthteller, and the kind of truth she deals in here will surely set you free."

Jennifer Dukes Lee, author of *It's All Under Control* and *Growing Slow*

"In *The Cost of Control* Sharon Hodde Miller explains that our need to control everything around us comes with a cost to our spiritual, physical, and emotional health. At a time when so many of us feel out of control, this book will help bring a necessary release. Sharon doesn't just give her advice, she gives you her pastoral presence. What if where you are right now is exactly where God can most lead you?"

Heather Thompson Day, author of *It's Not Your Turn*

the cost of
CONTROL

the cost of

CONTROL

WHY WE CRAVE IT,
THE ANXIETY IT GIVES US, AND
THE **REAL POWER GOD PROMISES**

SHARON HODDE MILLER

BakerBooks
a division of Baker Publishing Group
Grand Rapids, Michigan

© 2022 by Sharon Hodde Miller

Published by Baker Books
a division of Baker Publishing Group
PO Box 6287, Grand Rapids, MI 49516-6287
www.bakerbooks.com

Printed in the United States of America

Library of Congress Cataloging-in-Publication Data
Names: Miller, Sharon Hodde, 1981– author.
Title: The cost of control : why we crave it, the anxiety it gives us, and the real power God promises / Sharon Hodde Miller.
Description: Grand Rapids, MI : Baker Books, a division of Baker Publishing Group, [2022]
Identifiers: LCCN 2021056305 | ISBN 9780801094934 (paperback) | ISBN 9781540902221 (casebound) | ISBN 9781493436156 (ebook)
Subjects: LCSH: Control (Psychology)—Religious aspects—Christianity. | Influence (Psychology)—Religious aspects—Christianity.
Classification: LCC BV4597.53.C62 M55 2022 | DDC 155—dc23/eng/20220128
LC record available at https://lccn.loc.gov/2021056305

Author is represented by The Christopher Ferebee Agency, www.christopherferebee.com.

Baker Publishing Group publications use paper produced from sustainable forestry practices and post-consumer waste whenever possible.

23   24   25   26   27   28   7   6   5   4

To my parents, Rich and Debbie Hodde.

Whenever my life spun out of control,
you modeled God's steadfast love for me.
It has been so much easier to trust my heavenly Father
because you showed me what he is like.

Contents

Contents

Preface

In the late 1400s, in Heidelberg, Germany, there lived an alchemist, astrologer, and magician named Johann Georg Faust. The details of his life vary depending on the source, but he was well known as a trickster and a fraud. Frequently expelled from cities for performing horoscopes and sham miracles, Faust developed a reputation so widespread and notorious that Martin Luther was said to have speculated Faust had made a deal with the devil.

When he died in 1540, Faust's life quickly became the stuff of legend. Fifty years after his death, the poet and playwright Christopher Marlowe penned *The Tragical History of the Life and Death of Doctor Faustus*, a fictional version of the man's life that sealed his name in history.

In Marlowe's play, Doctor Faustus is a well-respected scholar who pursues knowledge as an obsession. Science, medicine, logic, theology, law—Faustus has mastered them all, but none of it is enough. He craves more knowledge and more power, and he dreams of all he can accomplish if he acquires them. So, Faustus turns to the only remaining option available to him: magic.

Soon he begins practicing the dark arts. One day while experimenting with spells and incantations, he summons a devil into his presence, and Faustus sees this as an opportunity. He dispatches the demon to its master, Lucifer, with specific instructions for making a deal. In exchange for his soul, Faustus requests twenty-four years of the demon's service, along with absolute power.

Lucifer happily agrees, and for twenty-four years Faustus is free to do whatever he pleases, though he uses the power to accomplish surprisingly little. As the term of their agreement draws to a close, Faustus wakes up to the reality of his own folly and becomes desperate to escape the consequences of their deal. He briefly considers turning to Jesus for help, but he ponders the option too long. In the final scene of the play, Faustus's soul is dragged off by devils and his body is torn to shreds.

This play is where we get the term "Faustian bargain." It has become the template for countless tales, each delivering the same cautionary message: When you make a deal with the devil, you lose much more than you gain.

Of course, that insight was not original to Marlowe. While Faust was the obvious inspiration for his work, one can't help but wonder if Marlowe was also influenced by a much older story, one that took place thousands of years earlier in a garden in the Middle East. It's a story that has been told again and again, repurposed and repackaged for thousands of years, because it contains a timeless lesson we are still reluctant to accept:

Whenever we reach for control to save us,
it always comes with a cost.

"No! You will certainly not die,"
the serpent said to the woman.

Genesis 3:4

Introduction

In March 2020, the world as I knew it ground to a halt.

I had spent the weeks prior in ignorant bliss, paying little attention to a new virus called COVID-19. In January of that year, my husband, Ike, and I took our church's college students to a conference with fifty thousand people. In late February, our family traveled to Disney World, where we milled around with thousands of other tourists. I noticed the occasional news story about cases popping up on the West Coast, but I brushed it all off as nothing. Like many others, I assumed it would be fine.

And then, just a couple weeks after we returned home from Florida, our entire school system shut down. We canceled our church's worship services "for two weeks," and we learned a new term called "social distancing." Before we knew it, we were buying masks, stocking up on hand sanitizer, and tumbling headfirst into the chaotic new reality of homeschooling our kids while leading our church remotely.

The whole thing felt like a draconian psychological experiment from the 1950s: *How do people respond when you threaten them with a strange virus and deprive them of human connection?*

As it turns out, not great.

In the immediate aftermath of the lockdown, I found myself combing through website after website trying to understand what was happening. I obsessively checked my temperature. I stalked our local news sites. I read every chart, every graph, every new piece of information I could get my hands on to try to anticipate what was next.

Meanwhile, our home life had devolved into a suburban *Lord of the Flies*. Ike and I divided our workdays in half so that one of us was teaching the kids while the other was working. This seemed like a clever plan at first, but instead it left us both feeling stretched to the limit and constantly behind. No matter how much I cut back on my responsibilities, I felt like I was leading our church badly and parenting even worse. During one particular stretch of months, I found myself feeling angry all the time. *Why won't my kids listen? Why can't they be quiet for just ten minutes while I send an email? Why haven't their teachers checked in?* I yelled at my children more than I had in their entire lives in this period of the pandemic, which means I also apologized to my children more than I had in their entire lives.

My experience, of course, was not unique. Every single one of us lost the comfort of our daily rhythms, while some lost their livelihoods and others lost family and friends. Our circumstances were different and our pain points diverse, but we all experienced some form of disorientation.

And yet, in spite of the fact that none of us had done this before, in spite of the fact that literally no one knew what was going to happen, none of this stopped people from dispensing advice. Heaps of it! When I scrolled through social media, I saw post after post about what we should or should not do. How we should or should not make use of this time at home. How we should or should not be responsible and safe. Some optimistically viewed the pandemic as a time of transformation. "Make the most of it!" "Emerge from your home like a transformed butterfly!" Others encouraged the exact opposite. "Do NOT make the most of it. Be gentle with yourself. This is a *lot*."

The flood of conflicting advice gave the world a manic feel. We were, collectively, trying to get a handle on the situation, and we were, collectively, failing at it.

All of this was revealing. The pandemic was exposing everything underneath our carefully curated exteriors. We each had a front-row seat to what was really going on in our souls and others'—mine included—and as challenging as it was in the moment, it also helped me connect the dots of a mental health trend I had been trying to understand for years.

The Mysterious Rise in Anxiety

Years prior to the pandemic, I began to notice a recurring conversation with people in our church, especially our college students. Our church is located in Durham, North Carolina, near three major universities, which means I am constantly meeting with students. For the last several years, I would go out to coffee or go on a walk or invite a few students over to hang out, and without fail the conversation would find its way to the topic of anxiety. Whether it was the anxiety of the student I was talking to or the anxiety of one of their friends, I began to realize that a startling number of our students were anguished about school, about getting a job, about life in general.

The American Psychiatric Association defines *anxiety* simply as "anticipation of a future concern,"[1] but it can take many forms with varying levels of intensity and impact, and I observed this spectrum in our students. The level of their anxiety ranged all over—from a vague gnawing to a constant pulsing stress to paralyzing, life-inhibiting panic attacks—but the trend was undeniable.

Once this pattern was on my radar, I began to notice it in other people too, like the young moms in my neighborhood or at my kids' schools. Women my age, with children the same age as my children, were wracked with anxiety about nursing their newborns, deciding where to put their kids in school, and generally doing what is best for their children. The start of kindergarten was a five-alarm emergency of overwhelm.

And then there were the pastors. I know a lot of pastors throughout the country who struggle with anxiety. I have spoken with some who had panic attacks before going on stage, and my own husband went through a season of ministry-induced anxiety as well. While serving as a young adult pastor at one church, there was a short period of time in which it was all Ike could do to show up for church on Sunday mornings.

Everywhere I looked, I saw anxiety. I saw it in the people in our church, I saw it on social media, I saw it in our politics, I saw it on the news. And once I saw it, I couldn't unsee it, so I wanted to understand what was going on and trace the threads back to what it all meant.

In my digging, I discovered a twenty-five-year study of individuals aged sixteen to seventy-one that found that between 1980 and 2005 anxiety levels had increased among men by 4.4 percent, and among women it had increased by roughly 6 percent. In young adults, however, the increase was far more dramatic. The anxiety levels among men aged sixteen to twenty-three had more than doubled, while the levels among women had tripled.[2]

The most recent research is even more alarming. Between 2011 and 2018 a survey of college students found that "rates of moderate to severe anxiety rose from 17.9 percent in 2013 to 34.4 percent in 2018."[3] In other words, the rate of increase is, itself, increasing.

What makes this trend especially puzzling is that young people are growing up safer than any generation prior. In her book *iGen: Why Today's Super-Connected Kids Are Growing Up Less Rebellious, More Tolerant, Less Happy—and Completely Unprepared for Adulthood—and What That Means for the Rest of Us*, psychologist Jean Twenge notices that, in contrast with boomer and Gen X children, who grew up "free to roam around their neighborhood," Gen Z kids are "supervised at every moment,"[4] and this supervision has paid off. Young adults born after 1995 are safer than ever. They are safer drivers and are less likely to get into car accidents.[5] They are also less likely to binge drink or use marijuana,[6] less likely to get into physical fights, less likely to be victims of homicide, and are generally more cautious and risk averse. Parents have succeeded in keeping this generation of young people very physically safe, which is what makes the rise in anxiety even more curious. Why are we more anxious when there is seemingly less to fear?

Because these statistics have been spiking so dramatically, I am not the only one who has noticed the trend. Psychologists and pastors alike have been trying to understand the sudden surge in anxiety. What we want to know is, *What has changed from before? What new factor is causing this?* The trouble is, there isn't just one answer. The problem of anxiety is multifaceted, complex, and cannot be boiled down to one thing. However, the pandemic did shed some light on it, because for so many of us, it brought out our anxiety in full force.

Prior to the pandemic, many of us were paying attention to the link between anxiety and pace of life. The rise in our collective anxiety coincided with the introduction of the smartphone, which led to the conclusion that we are overwhelmed by the speed and accessibility it provides. The flood of information, combined with the hyperconnectivity of the internet, is overstimulating and anxiety-inducing. The answer to this problem, logically, is to slow down and simplify.

I agree. This conclusion is right and helpful and important to understand. Spiritual disciplines, like silence and Sabbath, have anchored Christians for centuries, and they can anchor us now.

However.

The chance to slow down and simplify is, in some sense, what the pandemic gave many of us. While the nationwide shutdown threw our rhythms into disarray, destabilized our work/home balance, and hurled us into the steep learning curve of doing our jobs virtually, it also decreased the items on our daily schedules. It canceled our kids' extracurriculars, evaporated our overstuffed social lives, and all but eliminated our drive times. What it did not do was take our anxiety with it.

Instead, our anxiety spiked.

This response to the pandemic provided me with the missing puzzle piece to the question I had been asking for years. When the pandemic robbed us of certainty and predictability, it laid bare an idol that had been strangling us, invisibly, for years.

Why is our culture chronically anxious? One major factor is our relationship with control.

Naming the Problem

Our craving for control is not new. It dates all the way back to the very first humans, who chose their own sovereignty over God's. At the same time, our relationship with control has shifted and evolved because of our particular cultural moment, and that change has had consequences that *are* new. In the first two chapters of this book, we will look at this shift, and from there we will examine the primary ways we seek to control our lives and what that seeking is costing us. This book is composed of four major sections:

I. WHY We Control
II. HOW We Control
III. WHAT It Costs Us
IV. The REAL Power God Promises

The first section looks at the psychology and theology of control, the second looks at the primary tools of control, and the third examines the fallout. Only in the fourth section—the final two chapters—do I explain the solution. Based on this layout, you may notice that much of this book is devoted simply to naming and explaining the problem of control. That is an intentional decision, but I want you to understand why.

I am increasingly convinced we aren't giving enough time and attention to naming. By that I mean we aren't giving enough time to naming what is really going on in our culture, in our institutions, and in our hearts. Naming does not seem like much of an action verb, but there is no clearer example of the power of naming than in medicine.

Years ago I went to the hospital with excruciating pain in my stomach. It was so debilitating that the EMS workers found me groaning on the floor in agony, but once I arrived at the hospital, my doctor chalked it up to "just gas."

"Gas can be very painful," he explained to me somewhat patronizingly. "I bet you'll feel better in the morning!" I can't remember if he actually patted me on the head while he said this or if I am just remembering it that way, but after I restrained myself from screaming, "I have given birth, DUDE. This is not *gas*!" I got a second opinion and sure enough, it wasn't gas. It was gallstones. And once I named it correctly, I was able to treat it appropriately.

Our souls are the same. If we settle for superficial assessments ("It's just sin!"), we will address the problem superficially, and even incorrectly. This is why naming matters. I've heard it said that "when you name it, you tame it," and I have found that to be true. It is, after all, an insight that comes to us straight from Scripture. God's first act of naming was to name the light "day," and this action has forever intertwined "naming" with "light." Whenever we name something correctly, we bring it into the light, and only then can we see it clearly and engage it for what it is.

This naming cannot be rushed. When we jump to the solution without properly understanding the problem, it's easy to get the solution wrong. I could write a whole other book on all the problems we have misnamed, but for now, I will focus the majority of this book on naming. When we name and explain the problem of control correctly, much of the dysfunction takes care of itself. That is the sheer power of naming. It disarms the influences that are influencing us by bringing them out of the shadows and into the light.

PART I

WHY
We Control

1

The Illusion of Control

In 2009 a Christian talk radio host named Harold Camping predicted that the world was going to end. He based this prediction on a formula derived from Old Testament and New Testament events, which led him to the precise calculation of May 21, 2011.[1] Camping was so certain of his prediction that his network, *Family Radio*, spent millions of dollars canvassing the United States with warnings of a coming judgment. For two years they broadcast their predictions, purchased thousands of billboards, and translated booklets into seventy-five languages to get the message out.

The strategy was effective. Camping's followers prepared for the end by quitting their jobs, rushing into marriages, running up credit card debt, or conversely, giving all their possessions away. Among the most tragic stories was of a woman who attempted to kill her two daughters—aged eleven and fourteen—in order to spare them from witnessing the coming events. Thankfully they survived, but some of Camping's other followers did not. A handful of his disciples ended their lives in anticipation of the date.[2]

I still remember when all of this happened. It was a major news story that many of us followed with mournful compassion, while others simply mocked. But as the May 21 deadline came and went,

Camping's followers snapped out of their fanaticism and woke up to the reality that his predictions were wrong.

Years later I met a young woman whose family had been taken in by Camping's influence. She had been a college student at the time, and she dropped out of school to prepare for the predicted rapture. She remembers sending hundreds of emails to her friends, warning them to prepare. When the prediction failed, she was devastated. Her story is just one of many. Camping's false prediction resulted in catastrophic life upheaval, spiritual disillusionment, and years of therapy for many of the people who believed him.

To this day, there are still two aspects of Camping's movement that boggle my mind. To begin with, this was not Camping's first failed prediction. He had actually been wrong before! Nearly twenty years earlier, Camping calculated that the world would end on September 4 or 6, 1994.[3] When his initial prediction proved incorrect, that should have been the end of Camping's influence. It should have been clear to his colleagues and followers alike that he was a false prophet. Why he was ever given a second chance is beyond me.

But just as puzzling as his unearned credibility was his blatant contradiction of Scripture. In Mark 13:32–33 Jesus warns, "Now concerning that day or hour **no one knows**—neither the angels in heaven nor the Son—but only the Father. Watch! Be alert! For you don't know when the time is coming" (emphasis added).

Jesus is not ambiguous here. No one knows when the last day will come, not even the Son himself. That is the terrible irony of figures like Camping who scrutinize the dates and events in Scripture to crack the code of when the world will end only to overlook such obvious and direct words from Christ.

To those of us standing on the outside looking in, it doesn't make any sense. And yet, Camping was not unique. He belongs to a long line of Christians—some very well known!—who believed they could predict the end of the world. Going all the way back to the early church, here is just a sampling of the false predictions Christians have made about the end of the world:

- Hippolytus of Rome predicted the world would end in 500.
- The French bishop Gregory of Tours predicted the world would end between 799 and 806.
- The famous theologian Martin Luther thought the world would end no later than 1600.
- Christopher Columbus predicted 1658.
- John Wesley, the father of Methodism, thought it would be no later than 1836.
- Pat Robertson, who is best known from his role as host of *The 700 Club*, once predicted that the world would end in 1976.[4]

These are among the most prominent examples, but there are countless more. Despite Jesus's obvious warning, Christian history is chock-full of hubristic end-times predictions, all of which raise a nagging question: **Why does this keep happening?**

Why have so many Christians confidently predicted the end of the world, in direct contradiction with Jesus? For Pete's sake, Martin Luther might as well have had his motto, *sola scriptura* ("Scripture alone"), tattooed across his chest, and here he is, attempting to know something that Scripture explicitly tells us cannot be known. Clearly the temptation to predict the future is so strong that Christians have undermined their own ideals to discover it.

But why?

I recently listened to a podcast interview with church historian Sarah Hinlicky Wilson who discussed this exact topic—why so many Christians have made false predictions—and the answer she gave was this: **humans cannot tolerate uncertainty.**[5] When we look back on the history of the church, as well as the history of the world, we see humanity rebelling against the limitations of our own knowledge and control by claiming insight that God has not given us and asserting control we do not possess. We do

27

this, Wilson argued, because we find uncertainty and the lack of control simply "intolerable."

As it turns out, psychologists agree with Wilson. In fact, nearly a century of psychological research has confirmed her exact conclusion, and I want to share with you a very small taste of their findings. What follows is only a flyover summary, but it confirms the deep, human intolerance for uncertainty. When we cannot bear our lack of control any longer, we find ways to *feel* in control, and this coping mechanism is so common and widespread that psychologists have even given it a name.

The Psychology of Control

First, let's define exactly what we mean by the word *control*, because it is an umbrella term that can refer to many different things, including power, certainty, choice, and self-determination. The *Oxford English Dictionary* defines *control* as "the power to influence or direct people's behavior or the course of events,"[6] and the American Psychological Association defines it similarly: "authority, power, or influence over events, behaviors, situations, or people."[7]

These definitions are helpful but still a bit incomplete, because control is also about a feeling. It is the word we use to describe our sense of empowerment, or lack thereof.

In her book *It's All Under Control: A Journey of Letting Go, Hanging On, and Finding a Peace You Almost Forgot Was Possible*, Jennifer Dukes Lee digs underneath the textbook definition of control to capture the deeper motivation that drives it. She interprets the craving for control as believing "I'm safer and more secure if I'm in charge."[8] I like this description because it gets at the intangible quality of control. Control is not just about actual influence, but the *feeling* of power attached to it. So, for the purposes of this book, I am going to define control as "**the power to influence the world around us *and* the sense of empowerment that gives us.**"

28

Now that we have a working definition, I want to give you an ever-so-brief look at some of the research into the topic of control, because it explains a lot.

For much of the last century, psychologists have tried to understand why we crave control. One of the most significant, early voices in this research was a psychologist named Abraham Maslow, who famously developed the Hierarchy of Needs. First writing about this in the 1940s, Maslow described the Hierarchy of Needs as a "theory of human motivation," which was meant to explain why we do the things we do.

According to Maslow's Hierarchy of Needs, individuals are motivated to fulfill their most basic needs first, before they can even think about needs on any other level. As Maslow explained it, our most basic needs are Physiological (food, water, sleep) and Safety (shelter). Once these needs are satisfied, we are then motivated by the Need for Love and Belonging and the Need for Self-Esteem. Our final need, the one at the top of the pyramid, is the Need for Self-Actualization. We ascend to this level only once all our other needs are met.[9]

In this hierarchy, Maslow placed *control* on the level of Safety.[10] He believed that in order for us to feel safe, we require a basic level of control and predictability in our lives. If everything is unstable, chaotic, or dangerous, we will struggle to thrive.

A few decades after Maslow first proposed this theory, another psychologist named Ellen Langer revealed that our relationship with control is a bit more complicated, arguing that the human craving for control goes beyond our basic necessities. The urge to have control is so strong (and, one might argue, idolatrous) that we will *imagine control* even when we have none. Based on this theory, she coined the term the **"illusion of control,"** which explains all sorts of behaviors and practices, like superstitions. When an athlete wears the same socks during the playoffs, for example, he is inventing an *illusion of control* to cope with his lack of control over the games. This term also describes the subconscious behaviors we may not even realize we are engaging in but still give us a feeling of power. For instance, one study observed that casino players roll the dice harder for large numbers and softer for smaller numbers, as if rolling it harder or softer can control the number they roll.[11]

Langer wrote about the illusion of control in 1975, and since that time there have been scores of studies examining our desire for control, the ways we seek the feeling of it, and what happens when we fail to acquire it. The conclusion of these studies was that regardless of our actual control over a situation, we experience some benefit from simply believing we have control. Study after study has shown a link between feeling out of control and experiencing anxiety disorders.[12] But on the flip side, people who feel in control experience less anxiety, whether or not that feeling is tied to reality.

Now, if you just glazed over during those last few paragraphs, here is what it all boils down to: The illusion of control is powerful. If we *feel* like we are in control, it doesn't matter if we actually are. That is how influential the illusion of control is for the human imagination. Whether it is the foods we avoid to prevent cancer or the extensive plans we make for an upcoming vacation, these decisions are no guarantee of anything at all, but they make us *feel* better in the meantime.

What we've covered is only the tip of the iceberg. I could include many studies here, but I think it's fair to say that the desire for control is a human pathology. We as individuals and we as a culture crave control so desperately that we will reject reality and live in denial of our limitations for as long as we possibly can.

The Biblical Truth in These Studies

"All truth is God's truth." This was a favorite saying of my doctoral advisor, who frequently reminded my classmates and me that while we cannot add to the truths contained in Scripture, God has woven his truths into the fabric of creation. The research on control is a good example of this, because it bears witness to three biblical truths.

Humans Require Some Level of Stability, Security, and Physical Provision to Thrive

We see the importance of this in studies of child development. When a child's basic needs are not met, we call it "neglect." As a positive example, we see these basic needs being met in the garden of Eden. Adam and Eve didn't have *control* over the garden, but they possessed everything necessary to flourish.

The goodness of stability is also affirmed by the creation story in Genesis. God was not the author of chaos, but the organizer of it. When we look at his original design, we see order and stability. Conversely, when we yearn for order in our lives, that yearning is a spiritual nostalgia, an ache for a world that once existed and was ordained by God.

In short, it's okay to crave stability. God put that desire inside of you.

Humans Do Not Have Control, But We Do Have Agency

Agency is an important aspect of our human design. We will get into this concept in the fourth section of the book, but suffice it to say that we were not created to be puppets or prisoners. From day one, God instilled humanity with a power and an influence that he commissioned us to exercise in the world. Prior to the fall, we experienced this God-given capacity freely and perfectly; now we pant after it for a salvation it cannot provide. But we must not overlook the reality that our desire for control is also the distorted echo of something good.

Humans Are Prone to Self-Deceive

Again and again, these studies describe our stubborn refusal to face the truth. We would rather imagine a reality in which we have control—control over our future, our kids, our circumstances,

31

the end of the world!—than be honest with ourselves, which gives a whole new meaning to the term "my truth." When it comes to control, we are quite literally willing to invent a personalized version of reality.

This brings us back to Christian prophets and their false predictions. Why did they do it? Why did they continue to issue those prophecies, despite Jesus's expressed warning not to? Why did so many Christians believe Camping, even after his first prediction failed?

Because our resistance to reality is so strong, and our intolerance for uncertainty so deep, we will imagine control where there is none, and rebrand it as biblical insight.

What Happens When the Illusion Is Shattered

All of this leads us to the big, glaring problem with the illusion of control. While it seems harmless and even helpful (after all, it lowers our anxiety!), we cannot escape the fact that we are seeking refuge in a lie. The illusion of control allows us to retreat from reality, which feels great for a time, until the illusion is shattered.

Recalling Jean Twenge's research on Gen Z, and why the safest generation is also the most anxious, Twenge suggests the shattered illusion of control might be behind the growing levels of anxiety and emotional fragility in young people. She explains that children and teens today "spend more years fully aware that they are safe and protected in the cocoon of childhood. When they go to college, they suddenly feel unprotected and vulnerable." Boomers and Gen Xers, on the other hand, are "more likely to have experienced freedom before they went to college" and therefore "had a less jarring adjustment to make."[13] All of which leads Twenge to conclude: "We have what might be a trade-off. In keeping [our kids] physically safe, they are less emotionally safe."[14]

That "jarring" transition from illusion to reality is exactly what we experienced in the pandemic. When it first hit, it felt like everything in our lives had spun completely out of control, but the pandemic did not take away our control. It is not as if we had been living in a world where pandemics did not exist. Scientists had been warning of a pandemic for years. No, it was not the world that changed. What changed was our perception of the world. What the pandemic took away was not our power to predict, or our certainty about the future, but our illusion of those things, and this accounts for the surge of anxiety that immediately followed the shutdowns across the country. If the illusion of control lowers anxiety and that illusion was shattered, it is no wonder the entire world spiraled into a panic. We were confronted with a reality we had long worked to deny, and the pandemic exposed our spiritual lack of preparedness for it.

That is why, in the next chapter, we are going to pivot from psychology to theology. I am not, after all, a psychologist, so I want to be very clear that this book is not a sweeping solution to the problem of anxiety. Too often, leaders in the church offer spiritual solutions to psychological problems, but that is not what I am proposing. Human beings are multifaceted, which means we require different types of care. That is why we seek medical care *and* spiritual care. You don't go to your pastor for a broken back, but you might ask your pastor for spiritual guidance as you heal. Likewise, many of you reading this may need the expertise of a licensed therapist. If your anxiety is disrupting your daily functioning, I hope you will seek help from a trained and qualified counselor. But whether or not that is the appropriate step for you, my hope is to support you spiritually along the way.

On that note, there is one more biblical truth that the earlier research illuminates, and it explains why we struggle with control in the first place. Simply put, **this world is not as it should be.** Behind every struggle for control is a hurting person searching for peace in a chaotic world. That's all it really is, and God knows this, which is why he sent his Son to rescue us, once and for all.

In the meantime, as we wait on that rescue mission to be completed, our lack of control can be frightening. Especially whenever the illusion of control begins to crack and the reality of our vulnerability starts breaking in. When this happens—when we lose our jobs, when our plans don't work out, or when someone we love passes away—our human nature scrambles after another illusion to provide us with comfort and control, because this is how humans cope.

I will be the first to admit I know this temptation well. I understand the urge to retreat into an illusion of my own making, because I can feel so much more in control there. I have fought this impulse even while writing this book, which is why, as someone walking this path beside you, I want to commission you with this truth:

> When the news of the world is frightening, the diagnosis is discouraging, or the future foreboding, humans seek refuge in illusion. That is, as history tells us, what humans do.
>
> But we are not just humans.
>
> We are disciples.
>
> Not disciples of an illusion, but disciples of Christ.
>
> Which means our hope is not in an illusion.
>
> Our rescue is not in an illusion.
>
> Our peace is not in an illusion.
>
> And our joy is not in an illusion.
>
> To be a disciple of Jesus is to profess that **it is the Truth, not an illusion, that sets us free,** and this conviction is what distinguishes us as the people of God. As Old Testament scholar Walter Brueggemann once put it, the prophetic task of the church is to tell the truth in a society that lives in illusion.[15]
>
> That is our work and our hope. In a world that craves control, seeks refuge in a lie, and lives in utter dread of facing reality, we, the disciples of Truth, do not have to be afraid.

A Prayer for Illumination

Jesus, this world feels out of control. Very often, I feel out of control. I want to fix things, or know what is going to happen, and deep down, I do not believe I can have peace any other way. Open my eyes to the illusion of this thinking. Reveal to me the mirages of control that I breathlessly pant after, and instill in me a craving for the truth, rather than a lie. You say that the Truth will set me free, and I believe, but help my unbelief.
Amen.

Questions for Self-Examination

1. How do you cope with unpredictability or lack of control?
2. Do you think humans have any control at all? If so, what *do* we have control over?
3. In what area of your life do you most crave control right now?

2

How We Got Here

One afternoon my dad was sitting at the top of our driveway, hanging out with my kids. I came outside to check on them and asked my dad if he would like to join us for dinner. We were about to head to our favorite burger place, and I hoped he would come along. Instead, he furrowed his brow.

"I don't know if I have time. I have something at seven. It'll be rushed."

"It won't be rushed!" I objected. "Town Hall Burger is super fast!"

He looked unconvinced.

"It takes no time at all. You go to the counter and order, and they bring you your food."

He began to look annoyed.

I persisted. "There is absolutely no way it will even be tight. You will have tons of time left over."

My dad hemmed and hawed. Then he cut his eyes over to Ike, who had just wandered outside mid-conversation. He gave me a look.

"*What?*" I threw up my arms.

"You know what," Ike replied.

"No, I don't."

He walked over and jokingly herded me around the driveway like a sheepdog. "You push people." He chuckled. "You try to control what people do."

I wish I could tell you this anecdote is from my distant past. In truth, it happened last week.

As it turns out, writing a book about control does not extinguish the craving for it. As long as we live on this earth, we will all continue to wrestle with the urge, which is why researchers have given so much attention to it. The quest for control is universal.

However, the one question those studies cannot answer is, *Why*? *Why* do we struggle with control? Why have humans, throughout time, craved it? And why, in our current day and age, do we continue to crave control, even though we arguably possess more control than any generation before us?

When we look to Scripture, we find two answers to these questions. The first is very old, while the second is much newer.

We Inherited It

The blueprint for our own struggle with control can be traced back to our original parents, Adam and Eve, who are the first case study for why we crave control and what it costs us. From the very beginning, as seen in Genesis 1 and 2, Adam and Eve had everything they needed. They had food, water, companionship with God and one another, and they also had a high calling. There was no danger, uncertainty, anxiety, or fear. Their lives were defined by perfect peace and perfect unity. They experienced no bondage and no brokenness of any kind. They were totally and utterly free.

Adam and Eve lacked nothing essential to thrive. They sat atop Maslow's Hierarchy of Needs happily. Not an ounce of dread loomed on the horizon. They were flourishing just as vibrantly as the flora and fauna around them. Why, then, did they throw it all away?

Because, Scripture tells us, they were not ultimately in control. God had given them one limitation on their knowledge and their power: "You are free to eat from any tree in the garden; but you must not eat from the tree of the knowledge of good and evil, for when you eat from it you will certainly die" (2:16–17 NIV). This single boundary became the sticking point between their wills and God's, and seeing this, Satan pounced.

"No! You will certainly not die," the serpent lied. "In fact, God knows that when you eat it your eyes will be opened and you will be like God, knowing good and evil" (3:4–5).

With these words, Satan laid out the game plan for a scam he has been running ever since, the lie that any gap in our knowledge, any boundary on our power, or any limitation on our choice is something to fear, challenge, and resist. It's a deception that Adam and Eve fell for, and we are still falling for it today. Instead of entrusting ourselves to God's goodness, we believe our own control will serve us better.

It is the worst Faustian bargain of all.

This is the tragic irony of our original parents. In exchange for control, they lost their security. Just like our original ancestors, we struggle to grasp that the only time in human history when perfect freedom and peace existed in the world was not in the absence of boundaries, but within them. When we look at Genesis 1 and 2, we see that limitations on our freedom, our power, and our choice are an essential part of God's perfect creation, because we simply cannot handle the alternative. Our brains are not physically designed to wield unlimited control, and once again, research backs this up.

In his book *The Paradox of Choice: Why More Is Less*, psychologist Barry Schwartz describes this surprising finding:

> When people have no choice, life is almost unbearable. As the number of available choices increases, as it has in our consumer culture, the autonomy, control, and liberation this variety brings are powerful and positive. But as the number of choices keeps growing,

negative aspects of having a multitude of options begin to appear. As the number of choices grows further, the negatives escalate until we become overloaded. At this point, choice no longer liberates, but debilitates.[1]

The distinction Schwartz is making here is important. On the one hand, we must have *some* freedom, *some* knowledge, and *some* choice in order to thrive. The total absence of these things is the very definition of slavery. On the other hand, having absolute freedom, inexhaustible knowledge, and unlimited choice is not the secret to human flourishing. Instead, these things become a bondage of their own.

This distinction was absent from Adam and Eve's calculations. They were duped into believing "My world would be better if I was in control," which is quite literally a devil's bargain. What Satan did not want them to know and is still deceiving us with today is that **the more we seek control, the less control we feel**.

That is exactly what happened in the garden. Adam and Eve enjoyed perfect freedom and perfect peace *because* they did not possess absolute control. As soon as they rejected their limitations, their peace was replaced with anxiety, relational brokenness, and shame.

This disordered craving for control has defined nearly every family that came after, which means you and I have come by this struggle honestly. It's in our spiritual genes. Just like our first parents, we continually fall for the lie that more control can save us.

And just like our first parents, it only makes things worse.

That is the first reason we crave control. It's almost as if we cannot help ourselves, which means that none of us is alone in this struggle. It was injected into our spiritual DNA the moment sin entered the world.

That said, there is another aspect of our relationship with control that is relatively new, and that brings us to the second reason we yearn for control so desperately.

We Are Being Discipled into It

The word *discipled* might seem surprising here, but it helps to understand that the word *discipleship* comes from the root word *discipline*. A discipline, or habit, is a routine practice that shapes who we are, and our days are filled with them. Whether it is morning prayer or checking our phones, these daily, repetitive practices form us and influence us more than just about anything else we do.

And we belong to a society that "disciples" us into control. Or to be more precise, we belong to a society that disciples us into the *illusion* of it. Just consider, for a moment, some of your daily, weekly, and monthly habits:

- When you order a product online, you expect it to arrive within two days.
- When you want to watch a movie—any movie!—you stream it on demand.
- When you want to purchase a new vacuum, you read dozens of reviews to find the best model (or bargain!).
- When you want to know what the weather will be like in eight days, you check your weather app.
- When you want to eat at a restaurant without having to wait, you order ahead or have it delivered.
- When you want to buy salad dressing or mayonnaise or waffles, you go to the store and select from ten different brands to your precise specifications (gluten free, peanut free, GMO free, etc.).
- When you want to know what your child's cough means, you google it.
- When you need to find your way through a new city, you pull up your GPS.
- When you want to reduce the signs of aging, you buy serums and creams or have surgery.

40

- When you want your child to have a certain future by attending certain schools, you change your zip code.
- When you want to live longer, you eat healthy, exercise regularly, and get an annual physical. With the right finances, you can even repair or switch out any organs that aren't working.

At first blush, most of the behaviors on this list seem to be about instant gratification, and some of them are. But not entirely. What they *all* have in common is that they grant us the illusion of control. Thanks to technological advances like the internet, smartphones, satellites, modern medicine, air travel, and more, we have access to more knowledge, more choices, and more certainty than any generation before us. Together, these daily conveniences form expectations about the world and our mastery over it.

Now, please don't misunderstand me. Technology is a gift. In many ways, it is the grace of God in our lives. We are fortunate that more children survive childhood than ever before and that adults are living longer, thanks to the innovations of modern medicine. We are fortunate that we can feed more people, with more food, more efficiently. We are fortunate that we can make a trip in four hours that used to take weeks. And during the pandemic, we were fortunate to have technology that allowed us to communicate safely. When my great-aunt passed away in 2020, I said goodbye to her on FaceTime instead of in person, and that was devastating. But it was not lost on me that one hundred years earlier, during the Spanish Flu, humans did not have that option.

Freedom, knowledge, and choice are all good things, given to us by God. But when we possess an overabundance of them, it gives us a false sense of our own control.

And this is *new*.

One reason we know this is new is that the word for control does not actually appear anywhere in the Bible. There are no Hebrew or Greek equivalents that naturally translate to our word for control, although there are synonyms, such as restraint, mastery, rule, reign, or force. The closest we have is the Greek word *enkrateia*, which means "self-control," "self-mastery," or "temperance."[2]

What is especially noteworthy about all of these biblical synonyms for control is that whenever they appear in Scripture, they are almost always in reference to God.

Why?

Because control is a God category, not a human one. God can do whatever he wills, but we cannot. Not with the same unfettered sovereignty as he can. And for much of history, humans have understood this, because they lived it. They lived at the mercy of the weather, sickness, foreign powers, and the "gods." It was their undeniable reality. We, on the other hand, live in an unreality made possible by our technology, and because of this, we are retreating further and further into the illusion of control. In contrast with generations before us, our spiritual muscles of trust, of surrender, and of accepting our limitations have atrophied. Likewise, our senses of smallness and frailty feel terrifyingly foreign whenever we encounter them.

That does not mean we are the first culture to crave control. We're not. As we have already seen, our earliest ancestors shared a similar struggle. Adam, Eve, Abraham, Sarah, Isaac, Jacob, and every Christian leader who made a failed prediction about the end of the world—they all bear witness to our common desire for control.

But let me put it this way: we used to call people who promised certainty about the future a "cult."

Now, it's just our culture.

The Link between Anxiety and Control

I don't know about you, but when I scan the landscape of our culture's tendency toward anxiety, my first thought is not, *This is about control.* We don't always link these two factors together, but understanding the relationship between anxiety and control explains a lot about what we are seeing and experiencing.

It all begins with the simple fact that control creates anxiety. That's right, *creates*. Although we seek control as a solution to our anxiety, control also produces anxiety. It's counterintuitive on the surface, but the more we try to control something uncontrollable, the more out of control we feel. Then, to quell our anxiety, we seek to control even more.

This is a dynamic that author Steve Cuss explains in his book *Managing Leadership Anxiety: Yours and Theirs*. When we falsely believe that control will soothe our anxiety, and then we cater to that illusion, it triggers a spiritual domino effect inside us.

> When we do not get [control], we become very anxious. This anxiety blocks our awareness of God, makes us believe a lie, and keeps us from encountering grace. It teaches us a false gospel—that we need something other than Christ in the given moment to be okay. I think that is why so many people get stuck in their spiritual growth. . . . Instead of denying it or dying to it, they entrench it.[3]

This is a cycle we can all relate to, the ever-ratcheting up anxiety of trying to control something we cannot control. In *Harry Potter and the Sorcerer's Stone*, Harry, Hermione, and Ron fall into a tangle of vines called Devil's Snare, which only binds them tighter the more they strain against it.[4] Control is like this. The more we seek control, the more it exacerbates our anxiety rather than calms it. We are, in essence, trying to treat the sickness with its cause.

But here's the rub: The control-anxiety cycle used to be an individual struggle. Now, with the help of technology, we have structured our entire society around it. Thanks to the internet and our smartphones, our minutes and hours are filled with habits of control. Every day we are turning to the internet for certainty and our phones for predictability, and every time that we do this, the vines of anxiety tighten.

In his book *A Non-Anxious Presence: How a Changing and Complex World Will Create a Remnant of Renewed Christian Leaders*, Australian pastor Mark Sayers explains this cycle in a way I found so helpful. He distinguishes between "individual anxiety" and "systemic anxiety." He notes how often we address individual anxiety while completely ignoring the cultural form it is taking: "By classifying anxiety as a personal issue rather than a systemic issue, we place an enormous burden on the individual, who then must modify their personal lives to alleviate the suffering that anxiety brings."[5]

This distinction matters, because it explains why so many of our efforts to find peace are failing. We may make individual adjustments to our lives, like slowing down, observing the Sabbath, taking our anxious thoughts captive, or beginning and ending our days with centering prayer, but if we fail to acknowledge how the broader culture of control is shaping us—*discipling* us—we aren't addressing the whole problem.

So, what is the problem? **That our daily rhythms are rhythms of control, not rhythms of truth and reality.** And if we're going to talk reality, here is what is true: despite our technological advances, despite our acquired knowledge, despite our ability to predict and prepare, our control is still nothing compared to God's. We are living as if our control over the world has grown by miles when it has really only grown by inches.

The reality is, our world is just as unpredictable as it ever was. A friend of mine who is a psychiatrist recently said, "We have confused influence with understanding. We think that because we have a better understanding of the weather, or how viruses work, that we can control them. But we can't." And he is exactly right. Our increased knowledge has, ironically, caused us to lose touch with reality, which is why we are less and less spiritually prepared for it. And one symptom of this spiritual maladaptation is our increasing anxiety.

Breaking the Cycle

A few Christmas seasons ago the entire mail system slowed down, and thousands of packages were delayed. I had ordered some presents a month ahead of time, and they should have arrived within days, but instead they got stuck in the shipping jam. And how did I respond to this holiday hiccup? Coolly? Casually? Trusting in the goodness of the Lord? Of course not. I began tracking my packages like a bloodhound. One package arrived at my local post office but inexplicably sat there for days, so I refreshed the website relentlessly, as if doing so would magically entice the package to move. In the meantime, I started imagining doomsday scenarios in which we had no presents for Christmas.

"What if the presents don't make it?" *Refresh.*

"Will I need to buy whatever is left at Target on Christmas Eve?" *Refresh.*

"Will the kids remember Christmas of 2020 as their worst Christmas ever?" *Refresh. Refresh. REFRESH.*

By monitoring the progress of my packages, I was looking for some sense of control. Instead, I experienced the opposite. I ended up feeling even more frantic and helpless than before. I had turned to the illusion of control for help, and it failed, because it can do nothing else.

This is the paradox of control. The more we seek it, the less we feel it. We experience this anxiety in relatively harmless situations like the one I just described, but we experience it more acutely in others. In my church, some of the greatest anxiety I have experienced has resulted from my naïve belief that I could *make* people think or act a certain way. I was convinced that if I just explained something enough, or provided a person with enough scriptural backing, that I could walk them back from the self-destructive decisions they were making. This illusion has been the source of many sleepless nights and strained relationships because I overestimated my control over the situation and my control over the people.

45

As our technology advances and we gain an even greater sense of mastery over our world, our habits of control will only become more ubiquitous, and our connection to reality more frayed. So, what is the answer? If our culture is constantly oriented toward entrenching this illusion, how do we resist it? Is the answer to throw away our phones? Abandon the internet? Move to a monastery?

Thankfully, no. God has a different answer for us. But before we get to the solution, we need a fuller understanding of the problem.

A Prayer of Orientation

Search me, oh God, and know my heart. Test me and see if there is any anxiety in me. Grant me insight into my own craving for control and clarity about the daily habits that are feeding it. Uncover the idolatry of predictability that is whispering words of fear, and tune my ear to the true promises of your provision so that you might lead me in the way everlasting. Amen.

Questions for Self-Examination

1. Consider your daily habits. Can you name some "habits of control" in your life?
2. How do you respond when these habits of control fail? Can you think of any recent examples?
3. Can you think of a time when you tried to control a situation and it left you feeling more anxious?

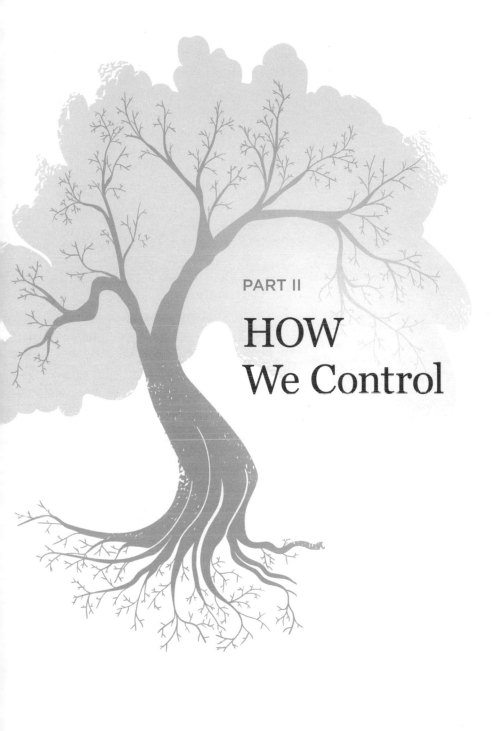

PART II

HOW
We Control

3

Knowledge and Information

You will be like God, knowing good and evil.

Genesis 3:5 NIV

For two weeks in the fall of 2018, I became a meteorologist. Not literally, of course, but emotionally.

In September of that year, Hurricane Florence was forecasted to plow through our state. For weeks we monitored its progress and prepared for the worst. At its most powerful, Florence was a Category 4 hurricane with sustained winds of one hundred fifty miles per hour, and our local weatherman warned that we might suffer a direct hit.

This forecast sent me into a tailspin for two reasons. The first is obvious: hurricanes are scary. I had lived through only one hurricane in my life, so I was not exactly a seasoned veteran. I wondered if we should pack up the kids and go stay with my parents in Charlotte, but there was another complicating factor that was also contributing to my stress. At the same time that the hurricane was bearing down on us, Ike and I were weeks away from launching our church. We were planning to hold a practice worship service on the very weekend Florence was scheduled to hit, and we weren't quite sure what to do.

As my imagination ran wild with all the worst-case scenarios, I did the only thing that gave me some sense of predictability. I tracked that hurricane's every move. I downloaded our local news channel's weather app, I clicked, "Yes, I DO want notifications!" and I became intimately acquainted with the Weather Channel's website. I followed each new development, in real time, 24/7.

And then, as the date of our practice service neared, something unexpected happened. The hurricane's path shifted. On a dime, weather experts changed all of their predictions and began speculating that it would skirt our area entirely.

In the end that hurricane never did hit us. In fact, we only experienced an ordinary amount of rain. So when I look back on those two weeks in 2018, the takeaway that really sticks out is this: hurricanes are *slow*. Not when you are standing inside of one, of course, but when you are sitting in front of your computer, in Durham, North Carolina, and that hurricane is out near Barbados. The hurricane will not speed up to anything more than an imperceptible creep, one painstaking millimeter at a time, and no amount of monitoring the weather map or clicking on the website will speed it up. If anything, it will only make the waiting worse.

This story is just one example of an insight I recently discovered about myself. One of the primary ways I cope with uncertainty is by turning to information for a sense of control, and as it turns out, I have been doing this for quite some time! When Ike and I first decided to start a family, I took all of my anxiety and uncertainty to the internet. Each month as I waited, I googled things like "tingling in my fingers" or "weird feeling in my stomach" to find out if these were early signs of pregnancy. Likewise, I have relied on the internet to shepherd me through mysterious medical symptoms like neck bumps or tingling in my elbow. Not surpris-

50

ingly, the outcome of this approach has always been the same. By turning to the internet to give me a greater sense of certainty, I became more anxious than ever.

I finally noticed this coping mechanism during the pandemic. I have never checked my local news more frequently than in those early months when the world was shutting down. I wanted to know exactly what was happening in my city, county, and state, and I devoured every prediction about what was going to happen next. It was the first thing I did when I woke up and the last thing I did before bed. In spare moments when I should have been playing with my kids, I turned to the news, to search engines, and to social media to give me answers, because it gave me some semblance of certainty about the future, if only for a fleeting moment.

That is, I now know, my pattern. I respond to the unknown by trying to know it, and the internet is always ready to help. I am not alone in doing this. Many of us react to uncertainty by researching it and gathering information in order to get a handle on it, and while we may not think of this as a form of control, it is arguably the very first one.

In this chapter, and in this section of the book, we are going to look at HOW we seek control, and we will start with knowledge and information. Neither works the way we think they will, and both do damage in the process.

Using Information to Feel in Control

To fully understand why we use information in this way, and how it affects us when we do, let's return to the scene of the crime—Genesis 3—where all our control issues began. It is no coincidence that the original story of control centers around a tree of "knowledge." We can trace our own distorted relationship with knowledge and information back to that moment. But before we get to that, I want to make one thing very clear: knowledge is a God-given good. The following argument is not against the virtue

51

of learning or the benefits of education. When our relationship with knowledge is rightly ordered, it produces humility and wisdom, which is why we ought to pursue it.

What we see in Adam and Eve, however, is an *idolatry* of knowledge. They desire a status and a power that God did not intend for them to have, and that is where they go awry. As soon as Adam and Eve eat of the fruit, the knowledge is immediately too much for them: "The eyes of both of them were opened, and they knew they were naked" (v. 7). Notice there is not even a moment of delay between their decision and its consequences. Adam and Eve are instantly overwhelmed by the newfound knowledge of their bodies and of their sin. Even worse, the peace and unity they once enjoyed is replaced with division and shame. All brought on by the possession of knowledge their souls were never designed to bear.

Anyone who has grown up in church knows this story well, and yet most of us fail to recognize that we are reenacting this very scene, multiple times a day. It is, after all, no small coincidence that the iPhone logo is a bitten apple. Every time we open our phones to check social media or the news, it's as if we are taking another bite of that forbidden fruit, ingesting far more knowledge and information than our souls can handle. Our smartphones give us access to an unprecedented level of knowledge and information, and it is overwhelming us just as much as it did Adam and Eve.

But that's not all that happened in Genesis 3. In addition to the shame and anxiety brought on by their newfound knowledge, their rebellion fractured their relationship with one another, and we are witnessing similar consequences today, though on an even bigger scale. Social media grants us an unprecedented level of knowledge about our friends and neighbors—quite literally the "knowledge of good and evil" in them—and this has caused widespread relational brokenness. Whether it is discovering a loved one's hateful opinions because of what they posted online, or that some of our friends went to a party or restaurant without us, we have access to an extraordinary level of knowledge about other peoples' actions and beliefs. And just like Adam and Eve, this knowledge is too much for us, which is why it causes anxiety in us and brokenness in our relationships.

Making this biblical connection helps us understand the shame and overwhelm we feel on a daily basis, but there is a second biblical analogy that can help us too. In Genesis 11, we read about an ambitious people who built a tower—which we now remember as the "Tower of Babel"—in an attempt to reach to the heavens and "make a name for [ourselves]" (v. 4). What they were really trying to do was make themselves equal to God, but it did not accomplish what they hoped. Rather than secure their power and unity, it divided and confused them. Ironically, it resulted in the very outcome they had hoped to avoid.

I cannot help but think of this story as a metaphor for our relationship with control—our phones functioning like tiny Towers of Babel that we use not only to make a name for ourselves but also to grant us access to all sorts of knowledge and power. Like the Tower of Babel, our phones allow us to stand high over the world, surveying everything that is going on all the time. But what we are discovering—and what we feel viscerally, pressing in on our souls every day—is that only God can handle this high-level knowing. Only he can know every shred of information there is to be known without becoming overwhelmed, distracted, and fatigued. He can do this because he is God. He is infinite. But we are not. We have limited love. Limited compassion. Limited ability to process. And limited emotional bandwidth. We literally cannot handle all the information we are taking in. We cannot handle the scope of the brokenness, and we become anxious trying to respond to it all.

And? That is okay. It is, in fact, the right order of things. What is broken about the world is not our lack of omniscience; what is broken is our unwillingness to accept it.

Knowledge is good. Information is good. Learning and curiosity about the world are all good. But no amount of information will satisfy our desire for certainty and control. When we turn to it to provide something it cannot, it will give us anxiety and strain our relationships instead, which leads us to the second way we misuse information.

Using Information to Control Others

In 2020 church leaders across the United States were faced with a triple whammy of upheaval: the pandemic, nationwide racial tension, and a polarizing presidential election. Our culture had fallen into a rut of deep partisanship, which meant that everything pastors did was interpreted through a political filter—every decision, every statement, every social media post. It made leadership choices precarious, to say the least.

The risk of misunderstanding was high, so Ike and I gave a lot of time and attention to explaining ourselves. We taught through the Scripture that was guiding our decisions, and we were transparent about the wise counsel and experts we were listening to. We knew this was necessary to instill trust in our people—and usually it did—but we also learned a very hard lesson during this season. No matter the scriptural exegesis, no matter the theological backing, no matter the data, the experts, or one's own record of integrity, you cannot convince people of something they do not want to believe.

Why? Because information is not nearly as powerful as we think it is.

In his book *A Failure of Nerve: Leadership in the Age of the Quick Fix,* author and family therapist Edwin Friedman described our limited influence this way: "The colossal misunderstanding of our time is the assumption that insight will work with people who are unmotivated to change."[1] As much as we wish it were otherwise, information has far less influence than we give it credit for. Downloading the "facts" into another person's brain is not going to magically change their minds, but I will be the first to admit this hasn't stopped me from trying. Whenever someone in my church, in my life, or in my comments online "needs to be corrected" (according to me), I am off to the races with all the arguments I could employ. In seconds flat, I can summon a hundred different talking points to convince them of the truth, if I could just sit down with them to explain it.

What time and experience have taught me, however, is that I am severely overestimating my own power to convince. Jesus himself hinted at the limited power of our arguments by concluding some of his hardest teachings with the statement, "Whoever has ears, let them hear" (Matt. 11:15 NIV). The implication is that some will *not* hear. They will not understand. Not because they cannot, but because they will not. No amount of convincing, no matter how compelling the evidence or airtight the logic, will move them. Not if they do not wish to be moved.

Research has also shown this to be true. When we use information to change someone's opinion, it can, in some instances, have the reverse outcome. The "backfire effect" is a term used to describe the doubling down that occurs when a person is presented with information that contradicts their own beliefs.[2] Rather than view the evidence objectively and adjust their beliefs accordingly, some people entrench their misbelief all the more. Further studies have shown that this phenomenon is especially likely to occur when belief is tied to *identity*. When new information feels like a threat to one's identity or way of life, people are much more motivated to reject it.[3]

Thanks to the last several years of ministry, Ike and I have learned to discern those who are receptive from those who are not, but I would be lying if I said I didn't still struggle with this form of control. Against all experience to the contrary, I still have a deep-seated belief in my own ability to convince. I can spend days ruminating, thinking about the perfect argument with all the facts and perspectives that I am convinced cannot be refuted. But if I were to do this in real life—come at people like an attorney instead of a pastor—it would backfire horribly. And it has. Like all forms of control, it doesn't work. It only feeds anxiety in me and strains my relationship with them.

Why It Doesn't Work

The reason knowledge and information cannot give us control is, on its face, rather straightforward. Knowing something does not mean you can control it. *Knowing* my husband does not mean I can *control* my husband. Knowing how hurricanes form in the ocean does not mean I can prevent them from coming. Understanding is not the same as influence, and it's as simple as that.

Then again, it's not that simple, is it? Information seems to promise us something we cannot resist—power and predictability— which is why we return to it for control again and again. With this allure in mind, I want to close out this chapter by looking at the two main reasons information cannot give us the control we crave.

Knowledge Positions Us Nearer to God, Not Equal to God

I love to learn. It is good and wise to pursue more knowledge, especially knowledge about God! Every corner of the universe contains new insight into the One who created it, and discovering this is a lifelong adventure. But sometimes we mistake the purpose of this journey.

To understand what I mean, imagine walking toward a skyscraper from a very great distance. When Ike and I were first married we had the amazing opportunity to travel to Dubai, where we were able to see the tallest building in the world. I will never forget the first time I laid eyes on it, from miles and miles away. I could see how it towered above all the other buildings, and that gave me some sense of its scale, but because I was standing at such a distance, it was still difficult to grasp its true size. If I closed one eye and held my thumb in the air, I could easily hide the whole building from my view. But as I drew nearer to the structure, its true scale came into proportion. I felt smaller and smaller, and once I finally stood in its shadow and strained my neck upward, I was awed and amazed at how tall it really was.

Education and learning are a lot like walking closer to a skyscraper. The more we learn about God and his creation, the more its true scale comes into proportion. The details become clearer. Our own sense of ourselves is corrected. Everything we learn gives us a fuller, truer picture of God and the world around us, and the right response to this is humility. As the saying goes, "The more you know, the more you realize how little you know."

At least, that is how it should be.

Unfortunately, our broken human nature often produces the opposite effect. Rather than humbling us and making us feel smaller in comparison with the depth and breadth of creation, we feel *bigger*. Knowledge puffs us up. We become arrogant and proud.

At its best, knowledge can inform, equip, inspire, delight, and ultimately lead us to worship. This is the kind of knowledge of God that Adam and Eve first possessed. But knowledge was never meant to supply us with a godlike feeling of control. It brings us closer to him in intimacy, but never equal to him in power. That is why frantically researching information fails to empower us when we use it to gain control. We are relying on knowledge to make us more omniscient and omnipotent when it is better suited to remind us we are not.

Persuasion Is about the Soil, Not the Seed

Knowledge and information have limited power, but does that mean we can never change people's minds? Do our words have any influence at all? Should we even bother to explain ourselves or attempt to convince people of anything?

The answer is of course! The book of Acts is a great example of the power of Spirit-filled persuasion. Both Peter and Paul delivered paradigm-shifting sermons that led to the salvation of thousands.

At the same time, the ability to change a person's mind depends on very specific conditions, which Jesus describes in the parable of the sower.

In Matthew 13, Jesus tells the story of a sower casting seed that falls on all sorts of soil. It lands on hard soil, rocky soil, thorny soil, and good soil, but it only grows well in one. Jesus then reveals that the soil is a metaphor for the condition of our souls. Only the soft and fertile heart will receive and cultivate the seed of the Sower, and this teaches us a difficult truth: If the soil is hard, it doesn't matter how much seed you throw at it.

This fact is crucial for how we think about persuasion. We can have all the best arguments in the world—the best research, the best experts, the best logic—but they will bounce right off that rocky soil. We can pelt the ground with all the studies and all the facts, but they will not penetrate an unreceptive heart. Sometimes they will only harden the soil more.

This has been a game changer for me as a teacher. What this parable ultimately taught me is that it is not the quality, the quantity, or the force with which I cast the seed that causes it to take root. The Sower scatters the seed generously, regardless of where it lands, and we are called to do the same. But—and this is a big *but*—we cannot make the seed take root and grow. Whether it is the seed of Scripture or the seed of data and information, growth is ultimately between the hearer and God.

Whenever we forget this, whenever we try to out-argue one another and force each other to change, it does not go well. Both parties only get angrier, more anxious, and more frustrated, and as we can see from our fractured culture, this dynamic is happening everywhere. It's happening around our family dinner tables, and it's happening in our churches. We are relying on information to do the heavy lifting of communication and transformation when God never meant for it to. As Matthew 13 reminds us, our time and energy are better spent discerning and interceding for the state of the soil in prayer.

The Most Powerful "Knowledge" We Have

One of the reasons we overestimate the power of knowledge and facts is that they are indeed powerful and God-given. Scripture is full of instructions, wisdom, and information about God and the world. At the same time the entire arc of God's Word bears witness to the failure of the Law to save. The knowledge of God was not enough to accomplish our restoration and transformation. It only highlighted how desperately we needed something more, and that, my friends, is why the Word became *flesh*.

In Greek, "Word" is translated from *logos*, which can also mean "reason," "logic," "principle," or even "teaching." When John 1:1 refers to Jesus as "the Word," John is describing Jesus as the "logic of God." He is the knowledge of God *embodied*, which means Jesus is the "knowledge" we truly crave. Jesus is the only "knowledge" that will give us the peace and security that control cannot provide.

As the "logic of God," Jesus is also the blueprint for how we influence and communicate with others. We can dispense information all the livelong day, but the thing that really moves people, and connects them and changes them, is not our human logic, but Christ in us. This, not information, was God's answer to heal the world. And so it must also be ours.

A Prayer of Confession

Good Father, I confess to you the oldest sin of humankind: using knowledge to control. I confess my desire to know the future, rather than entrust the future to you. I confess that I run to information for refuge, instead of running to you. I confess to using knowledge to coerce or manipulate

*others, instead of praying and bringing the matter to you.
Thank you for the gift of knowledge—that we can know
and learn—but restore me to a right relationship with it.
You alone are God, and there is no other who can make my
feet steady and secure like you.*
Amen.

Questions for Self-Examination

1. What is the difference between wisely acquiring information and using information as a tool for control?

2. When was the last time you researched something in order to feel a sense of control over a situation? How did it make you feel?

3. In what ways do you find yourself using information to control or change other people?

4. Think of a time when new information opened your eyes and changed you. What about that situation softened your heart and made you more receptive?

4

Power

The devil took him to a very high mountain and showed him all the kingdoms of the world and their splendor. And he said to him, "I will give you all these things if you fall down and worship me."

Matthew 4:8–9

About a year after Ike and I launched our church and it had started to grow, we began to notice a problem: *me*.

Ike is the lead pastor of our church and I am the teaching pastor, but because we cofounded the church together (and because we are married) I was making a lot of leadership decisions in the beginning. If there was a question about the worship service, I would answer it. If there was a problem with guest services, I helped solve it. Throughout that first year, I was speaking into every area of the church, which was necessary and worked well until our church began to grow. The bigger we became and the more staff we hired, the less I knew what was going on in every area of our church and the less it made sense for me to share my opinion. This became especially clear when I accidentally gave input that contradicted Ike's, creating confusion among our staff.

It took time, but what I had to realize was that many people saw me as a proxy for Ike. They assumed I knew what he knew and that my opinion was consistent with his. Because of this, they came to me with questions I was not actually equipped to answer, and I needed the self-awareness to say, "That's not my job" or "I simply don't know."

The problem was, I didn't want to do that. I didn't want to relinquish speaking into the aspects of our church that I cared about, especially the areas that I used to lead myself. I wanted to retain some level of control in our church, and because of my position as Ike's wife, I had the power to make it happen.

Power is probably the most obvious and common form of control, and it encompasses a whole host of control-related dynamics like manipulation, coercion, privilege, and force. Each of these forms of control is distinct, but if I could summarize their common, overarching relationship with power, I would put it rather simply: Power-based control is when we exert control simply *because we can*. Because this is not how we typically talk about "power," here are a few examples of what I mean:

- When a boss requires his employees to work crazy hours and meet ridiculous expectations, he does it because he can.
- When a parent berates her children with excessively harsh discipline, she does it because she can.
- When the leader of an organization creates a culture of fear through punishing criticism, she does it because she can.
- When a husband or wife inappropriately influences their spouse's workplace leadership, they do it because they can.

- When a Hollywood executive forces young actors or actresses to endure abuse in order to land a role, the executive does it because they can.
- And when American slave owners bought, sold, and tortured African people like animals, they did it because they could.

Whenever we control someone or something, simply because we can, we are exercising *power*.

I know this is an unusual way of talking about power, but I chose this description to underscore the reality that it is something we all possess. When we think of the "abuse of power," we tend to imagine wealthy, high-profile leaders overseeing wide-scale corruption, not our own ordinary choices. But that is exactly what is happening when we explode on our kids to silence them or when we pressure our subordinates to work an unhealthy number of hours. It is also what is happening when I coerce my husband to confront someone when he doesn't want to. What I am doing is taking advantage of my power in our marriage in order to get the result I want. And I am doing it simply because I can.

Power is perhaps the most tempting form of control because it is the most effective. Unlike knowledge and information, which very often fail to accomplish what we hope, power is the closest thing we have to actual control over people and circumstances in our lives. Abusers *do* control their victims. Human traffickers *do* control the people they enslave. In toxic work environments, employers *can* control their employees. Even in our daily lives, we have plenty of opportunities to engineer our desired outcomes. Whenever we pressure someone into a commitment they can't say no to, or force our children into activities or a career path they would not choose for themselves, we are exerting our control over them. This is the same kind of power that positioned Sarah to manipulate Abraham and mistreat Hagar (Gen. 16). It is this same kind of power by which Laban demanded seven years of service from Jacob. And then seven more (Gen. 29)! And it is this same kind of power that enabled Joseph's brothers to sell him into slavery and get away with it for years (Gen. 37). Power comes in all forms, some big and some small, but in whatever capacity we can access it, it gets the job done.

Unless, of course, that "job" is reflecting the character and ways of God and imitating his own use of power.

In that case, it fails miserably.

God's Use of Power

In her book *Redeeming Power: Understanding Authority and Abuse in the Church*, author and psychologist Dr. Diane Langberg explains that God gave power to all humans. She writes, "Every human life is a force in this world. Our influence pours out perpetually."[1] This design is evident from the very beginning. God created Adam and Eve in his image (Gen. 1:26), which means we possess power like God does, but we are also called to wield power as God does. Langberg explains, "God gave human beings power in order that they might bear God's character in the world."[2]

This point then raises a question: What does it look like to use our power in God's "image"? How can we use power to reflect God's character instead of to control? One answer comes to us directly from the garden. In Genesis 1 and 2, we see God using his power almost exclusively for two things: **to create and to empower.** He created the world, he created people, and then he empowered them to exercise dominion in the world. After that, he instructed them to "be fruitful and increase in number" (1:28 NIV), which meant repeating what he had just done. *Create and empower.* That is one way we use our power the way God used his.

The problem with control is that it undermines this vision. Rather than use our power to empower others, control disempowers and dominates. And rather than use our power to imitate

God, we use it in an attempt to be equal with God, which is the irony of Adam and Eve. As Dr. Langberg puts it, Adam and Eve "wanted what they were meant to have: likeness to God."[3] But because they also wanted to be equal to him, they became less like him in the end.

With that in mind, I want to look at five ways we seek control through power, because we often fail to recognize we are even doing it. This list comes directly from Dr. Langberg's writing, and although I will not cover all the forms of power she does, I believe these five are the most common.

Verbal Power

My husband calls it "loading my ammunition." Sometimes when I am upset with him, I withdraw to another part of the house and sulk about in silence while internally mounting an attack. As soon as he makes the mistake of asking me what's wrong, I blast him. *Bam bam bam bam bam bam bam.* I pelt him with such an overwhelming barrage of complaints and accusations that he is too stunned to even know what hit him. And it works.

Early in our marriage this was one of the most effective means I had for getting my way. I am a writer and a preacher, so I am strong with words. It is a gift God gave me. But like any gift, it is a double-edged sword that can unleash a great deal of harm. I can slice and dice a person. I can light social media on fire. I can also argue any person into a corner. I have a lot of power on the tip of my tongue, which I have sometimes used as a form of control.

The problem is, I am not exercising control in the way that I think I am. When it comes to verbal power, Scripture tells us that it can be used in only one of two ways: building or destroying. Proverbs 18:21 says, "Death and life are in the power of the tongue." Notice that there is no middle ground here. We can use verbal power to imitate God, who literally *spoke* the universe into existence, or we can use our words to destroy, as James vividly warns: "Though the tongue is a small part of the body, it boasts great things. Consider how a small fire sets ablaze a large forest. And the tongue is a fire" (3:5–6).

This fork in the road—between building and destroying—is always before us, and because of this, it needs to be a part of our calculations when we want to "win the argument." In the example of my husband, I might ultimately get my way, but I'll do great damage to our relationship in the process.

That said, the destructiveness of verbal power is not always so obvious and direct. There are subtler ways we rely on it to control, and one of the sneakiest is gossip. Most of us do not equate gossip with power, but very often that is exactly what it is about. Gossip is a weapon for those who feel powerless. We know we can't control our boss or that politician or even that friend, but we can control their reputation. And so, with one whispered conversation veiled in the tone of "concern," we light the match that burns their name to the ground.

The majority of us are far too cavalier with our verbal power, but it is worth noting that Jesus never was. I suspect this is the very reason he rarely engaged in debates, instead speaking in parables and answering the religious leaders' questions with more questions. He almost never spoke in anger. Jesus knew the power of his words to cut *unnecessarily*, which is why he primarily used them to teach and to heal, rather than to control.

If we claim to follow him, that is our precedent. When we use our words to control—whether it is our family members, our employees, or strangers online—it may or may not "work," but one thing is for sure: we will not sound like Jesus at all.

Emotional Power

One of the reasons Jesus's teachings were so powerful was not only because of what he said, but how he said it. His arguments were convincing, not just because he knew the Law better than anyone, but because of the heart behind his words. Jesus very obviously cared. He loved people. He felt deep-down-in-his-gut compassion for them. He wept when they wept, and he rejoiced when they rejoiced. He was not aloof or emotionally indifferent. He was intimately attuned to people's pain.

Because of this, Jesus exemplified the tremendous influence of emotional power, which often works hand in hand with verbal power. Dr. Langberg writes, "Emotions can be used to comfort another with empathy or to control what people say and do, often intimidating and silencing them. The power of anger or rage can terrify a human being, with or without words."[4]

While Jesus used emotional power to bless and build up, we have all experienced the opposite at some time or another. The weight of shame, guilt, and fear is daunting. It motivates behavior modification unlike almost anything else. And because of this, we sometimes feel tempted to use these harmful forms of emotional power, especially within our own families. Nothing packs a punch like the withering words, "I am disappointed in you," which are not always an expression of sincere heartache, but an emotional power play on another.

Emotional power, like verbal power, is common and ordinary. It is not a power reserved for the rich and famous, but a power accessible to us all. We very often use it without even realizing. In *A Failure of Nerve*, Edwin Friedman makes a strange argument about power dynamics in a group. He explains that the most anxious person in the room is often the most powerful. It's a counterintuitive idea, but you have probably experienced this in family gatherings or meetings. The most anxious or most reactive person in a group ends up driving the direction and the tone of a conversation, because the rest of the group starts working together to appease them. This dynamic likely transpired in businesses and city councils all over the country as each entity considered its response to the pandemic. When a single board member's voice begins to rise with fear, the entire dynamic of the group shifts toward quelling that individual's anxiety.

That does not mean emotion is inherently manipulative. It is not. Jesus frequently responded out of emotions like compassion and sorrow. But there is a reason God repeatedly warns us not to fear. While our emotions reflect his very image, *fear* is a form of emotional power we must never take up. Intentionally or unintentionally, our anxiety has the power to influence people around us, and rarely in the direction of Christ.

Physical Power

Dr. Langberg calls this "embodied power," and while we are very aware when we are being threatened by it, we tend to be "less aware of what our own presence communicates to others."[5] Looming closer, folding your arms, clenching your fists, avoiding eye contact. These quiet physical cues communicate volumes, and while this is especially important for men to understand, as they may not realize the ways their presence is intimidating to women, it is also important for parents and adults who work with children. It is quite easy to control children with our physical presence, or a very firm grip, but it cannot be overstated that Jesus *never* did this. Even at his angriest, Jesus never got in someone's face and stared them down. He did not become physically violent, and he even rebuked Peter when he did. Instead, Jesus's physical presence was the location of love, service, and self-sacrifice, and that—not physical intimidation—was how he motivated others and changed the world.

Authoritative Power

The power that comes from being in authority derives from several primary sources—education, expertise, and institutions—and like the other forms of power, it can be used for good. Doctors, for example, use their authority to make difficult but necessary calls and guide us toward wise medical decisions. Teachers use their authority to educate, invest in, and build up their students. Pastors use their authority to speak life and hope into their church members' lives. However, this power can have a shadow side. Dr. Langberg warns that "we often trust others in positions of authority because we assume that those with knowledge, intellect, and skill must be trustworthy," and this "increases the likelihood that a leader will be granted unfettered, sometimes automatic authority by the people they lead."[6]

This unfettered power has enabled verbal, emotional, physical, sexual, and spiritual abuse by authorities, but in many instances, the misuse of authoritative power is far less obvious. For most of us who possess some sort of authority—whether it is as a manager at work or a parent in our home—we begin to misuse our power after a subtle shift occurs inside our hearts: away from the care of others and toward the protection of ourselves. God-given authority exists for the good of those under it, but as soon as we prioritize our comfort or our convenience over the good of others, authoritative power goes off the rails.

Speaking personally, I often misuse my authoritative power in my everyday life as a mom. Ike and I are the primary authorities in our kids' lives, which is generally for their good. I tell them not to touch the hot stove or run into the street or eat food they found on the ground, and because they listen to me, they don't get hurt or sick. But if I am distracted by my phone or tired or trying to get work done and they interrupt me, I will raise my voice and dole out an excessively harsh consequence. When I do this, I am not using my authority for their good but for my convenience. I simply want them to stop bothering me.

It is critical for those in power to be honest about this temptation, because authority has an incredible amount of power to harm. Remember, when we use control to fix things, we end up breaking them even more, and this is especially true when paired with authoritative power. Even the most delicate manipulation by an authority can be devastating, because the misconduct becomes associated with whatever the authority represents. When we misuse or abuse our position of authority, we are not just damaging our personal relationship with a person, we are also damaging their relationship with family, doctors, the church, or even God.

Perhaps this is why Jesus was so hard on religious leaders. When you use your authority as "God's anointed" to control people, the fallout is catastrophic.

Spiritual Power

I sort of hate to admit this, but one of my all-time favorite television shows is *Hart of Dixie*, starring Rachel Bilson. The series is about a New York City doctor who moves to Bluebell, Alabama, to work at her father's practice. There she encounters a town of eccentric characters. One of those is Reverend Mayfield, a classic small-town pastor who knows everyone by name and is unflappably friendly. I generally like his character because he is a good husband and an unconditionally loving presence in the town, but there is one thing about him I wish I could change. Sometimes when he is trying to convince a parishioner to help with an event or serve in the church, he cheerily twists their arm with the words, "Don't do it for me. Do it for the big guy!"

It sounds benign, but it makes me cringe every time. While the character in the show is harmless enough, this form of manipulation by a spiritual leader has, in different circumstances, utterly shipwrecked people's faiths.

The power in "spiritual power" derives—or seems to derive—directly from God himself, which is why it can be wonderfully transformative or wickedly toxic. Some of the most life-changing experiences I ever had were in the company of Christian leaders who were the "aroma of Christ" to me (2 Cor. 2:15 NIV). When I was with them, I felt totally seen and loved. I felt cared about and listened to. I felt dignified and safe. Whether it was a pastor or a Christian author, they leveraged their spiritual power to invigorate my imagination about what the living, breathing Jesus was like.

Unfortunately not everyone has this experience. Some people have experienced spiritual power in harmful and even demonic ways. Spiritual power can be used to manipulate, to extort, and to steal from the poor. It can be used to bully and abuse. It can be used to build Babel-like empires, and it can be used to spiritualize the shaming of people who do not conform. At its worst, spiritual power is used for evil. It attaches the name of God—who is meant to be our refuge, our strong tower, our comforter, our restorer, our hiding place—to the darkest, vilest acts. In doing so, it breaks the very tools God gave us to heal, turning Scripture and the church into a minefield of trauma, which is why this form of abuse is nothing short of satanic.

That said, we can unintentionally misuse spiritual power in less severe ways. I recently spoke with a friend whose former pastor advised her not to leave the church because, as he put it, "he was responsible for her." I imagine this man's heart was entirely in the right place, but this seemingly innocent form of pressure highlights the precariousness of spiritual power. Even if our motives are just *slightly* off, just *slightly* selfward, and we attach God's name to them, we can distort someone's entire perception of God.

This is what made Jesus's life and teaching so remarkable. Jesus's use of spiritual power did not distort but *clarified* who God is and what he is like. One reason for this clarity—besides Jesus being God—is that his message never became entangled with selfish motives. His reasons were always pure, always for our good. When he rebuked, it was about so much more than being right. Rather than force us to follow him, he wooed us with sacrificial love.

Rethinking Power

One of the reasons Christians get enmeshed in worldly affairs is that we think we can use the tools of the world, as long as we use them "differently." We want to use wealth, but "differently." We want to use anger, but "differently." We want to use power, but "differently." We brand these approaches as "redemptive" or "Christian," but Jesus displayed no interest in attaining worldly power. Jesus could have become a king and done a lot of good. He could have amassed tremendous wealth and done a lot of good. He could have imposed his will on the world and done a lot of good. But that is not what Jesus did. Instead of exercising worldly power "for good," he surrendered his power. In doing so, he completely redefined what power is. For Christians, power is a person. Jesus Christ. This means our own power is found not in force, but in our intimacy with our Savior and our likeness to him.[7]

Does this mean there is never a time to intervene? Never a time to rescue or thwart the schemes of the wicked? Of course not. God uses his power for good, and so should we. At the same time, the consequences of the fall and the entire arc of human history caution us to be clear-eyed about the temptation that power poses and how desperately our flesh would rather trust in power than in God. That might be why Jesus modeled a completely different relationship with power. Although Jesus will, one day, return to rule over all creation, he made the intentional choice during his life on earth not to reign but to die, and then he invited us to do likewise. That—not the wielding of worldly power, even for "good"—is the primary paradigm Jesus gave us.

Knowing what to do with the power we have available to us requires great discernment. But again and again, we must remember it was Jesus's self-giving sacrifice, not his dominance, that saved the world. If laying himself down was enough to overcome evil and death itself, then it must be enough for us too. We must be known as the strange and radical people who do not need control and do not rely on worldly power, because we trust the One whose ways are higher than our own.

A Prayer of Confession

Jesus, you know the temptation of power. You experienced the allure of its promises just as acutely as I do every day. But too often I do not make the choice you made. I do not reject worldly power, but instead I rely on it. I trust it. I ask it to give me the control I crave. And whether or not it works in the short term, it betrays in the long. I confess my reluctance to trust you and your kingdom ways. I confess my desire to do things myself and to put myself in your place. Help me reject the broken power of the world and its false promise of control, and transform me into your likeness so that I can be powerful in all the ways that you, not the world, measure power.
Amen.

Questions for Self-Examination

1. In what areas of your life do you have power?
2. Which forms of power do you find yourself turning to for control?
3. Do you think it is ever okay to use your power to control others? Why or why not?
4. Can you think of a time you used your power to engineer an outcome and it went badly?

5

Money

Those who trust in their riches will fall.

Proverbs 11:28 NIV

"Tell them to name their price. Everybody has a number!"
Believe it or not, this sentence came out of my mouth in
a staff meeting. Our church has grown and stretched beyond the
limits of our current location, so we have been looking for other
options for months. One especially convenient option had been
closed to us for years, but when the door began to open a bit, my
shrewd, wheeling-and-dealing boss-lady side came out. I did not
know this part of me existed until she was making hard-nosed
suggestions like "Go above their head and call their boss!" and
asking spiritual questions like "Who would turn down *MONEY*?"
As if money—not the miraculous power of God—is the solution
to all our problems.

The temptation to rely on money as a means of control is a
powerful one, but it is also one of the subtlest. Like the other forms
of control we have examined, we don't always realize we are relying on it, and I can speak to this from experience. I grew up in a

home where we always had more than we needed. We lived in a nice house. We took nice vacations. I attended a very good school. When I turned sixteen and got my driver's license, I was given a car that I did not have to pay for on my own. Because of all this, things in my life just *worked out*. I could go to whatever college I chose, because finances were not an obstacle for me. I was able to put all my focus on my schoolwork, because I didn't have to get a job. That didn't mean everything was easy or that I never faced hurdles, but none of those hurdles were financial.

If you had asked me whether I trusted too much in money, I would have said no, but in truth, I had no ground to stand on. When you grow up with wealth, you go through life with an invisible safety net underneath you at all times. This made it hard to know how much of my faith's foundation was standing on Christ or trusting in the net. I wasn't able to see myself, or my faith, clearly until this safety net was gone, and if my response to our church's location search was any indication, I trusted in money quite a lot.

Most people, of course, do not grow up as I did. The majority of the world, in fact. Most people have experienced financial lack or instability during their lifetime, so before we dig in to the relationship between money and control, I want to ground this conversation in God's heart for those in need. God's orientation toward the poor, the hungry, the homeless, the orphan, the widow, and the vulnerable is most certainly one of compassion.

> The one who oppresses the poor person insults his Maker, but one who is kind to the needy honors him. (Prov. 14:31)
>
> Kindness to the poor is a loan to the LORD. (Prov. 19:17)
>
> A generous person will be blessed, for he shares his food with the poor. (Prov. 22:9)
>
> And if you offer yourself to the hungry, and satisfy the afflicted one,

then your light will shine in the darkness,
and your night will be like noonday. (Isa. 58:10)

"If you want to be perfect," Jesus said to him, "go, sell your be-
longings and give to the poor, and you will have treasure in heaven.
Then come, follow me." (Matt. 19:21)

These verses only scratch the surface. The Bible is positively
brimming with God's care and concern for our needs, which means
if you grew up in financial insecurity, or if you are living in it now,
your desire for money is not a sign that you struggle with control.
It is a sign that you live in a broken world.

That truth is a necessary prerequisite for this chapter. The desire for "enough"—enough food, enough money to pay the bills,
enough margin to splurge on your loved ones—is not wrong or
sinful. It is a holy yearning for the paradise you were created to
inhabit, a paradise where there was always enough. That world is
behind us, and it is also ahead of us, but your soul feels the dis-
sonance of this in-between place. And that is okay.

With that in mind, Scripture also focuses a lot of time on warning about our fractured relationship with money.

If wealth increases,
don't set your heart on it. (Ps. 62:10)

Don't wear yourself out to get rich;
because you know better, stop!
As soon as your eyes fly to it, it disappears,
for it makes wings for itself
and flies like an eagle to the sky. (Prov. 23:4–5)

Whoever loves wealth is never satisfied with income. (Eccles. 5:10)

No one can serve two masters, since either he will hate one and
love the other, or he will be devoted to one and despise the other.
You cannot serve both God and money. (Matt. 6:24)

That third verse is a WHOLE sermon. For any of us who claim we do not trust our money too much, Ecclesiastes evades our self-deception by asking an entirely different question:

Are you satisfied with your income?

Is your current income enough for you, or do you find yourself daydreaming about how much better, or easier, your life would be with just a little more?

These questions get at the relationship between money and security, a relationship that falls on a spectrum. On one end, money is the provision of a basic need; on the other end, money is a form of control. The point at which our relationship with money shifts from a "healthy need" to a "control need" is when our basic needs are met but our hearts don't reflect it. I know families who make six-figure incomes, live in giant houses, and send their children to private schools, and yet they still relate to money with a poverty mentality. Money is their constant focus and a steady source of anxiety and stress. They have plenty, but it never *feels* like enough. This leads us to the first way we use money to control. When we cling to money for stability and predictability, and live in dread of losing it, we are using money to feel in control.

Using Money to Feel in Control

Jesus talks about money a lot. More than just about any other topic, in fact, and his reason is twofold. The first is our propensity to trust in money more than just about anything else. The second is our unwillingness to be honest about it.

As I already admitted, it was difficult to acknowledge how deeply I trusted in money, partly because I couldn't perceive it. When I imagined someone who trusted in their wealth more than in God, I imagined other people: The Christian who never tithes. The wealthy churchgoer who lives extravagantly but is stingy about giving. The husband and wife who both have high-income jobs but are still constantly stressed about their finances. It is so easy to diagnose in others, isn't it?

But both Scripture and research tell a more universal story. Studies show that the more money one accumulates, the more likely they are to become attached to it. With few exceptions, study after study has shown a "decline in charitable giving relative to income," suggesting that "lower income groups are relatively more generous than higher income groups."[1] Another study found that "'higher status' people are less likely to give money when it is earned" rather than inherited. Defined according to social, economic, and educational attainment, "high status" individuals were less generous than "low status" individuals because they "wanted more control over the money they had earned, so they contributed less."[2] All of which means Ecclesiastes is right. The more you have, the less you act like it.

These studies show that our idolatrous attachment to wealth is a human condition, not limited to the wealthy few. And yet, stunningly, we still struggle to be honest about this, which is probably why Jesus talked about money so much. He was helping us see what we will not see on our own, a lesson that is nowhere clearer than in his interaction with the rich young ruler in Matthew 19. In this particular encounter, a young man approaches Jesus with great confidence in his own righteousness. He is a follower of the Law. He has kept the commands. He has not committed murder or adultery. He has honored his father and mother. He has loved his neighbor as himself. His wealth—in his mind—is unrelated. Perhaps he even gives a little bit of his money to charity, in which case he may believe that his wealth actually *helps* him to better *fulfill* the Law.

In this brief exchange, Jesus provides a lesson for us all, a lesson about how easily we will adjust our theology to fit our wealth. I have heard entire sermons doing this acrobatic work, arguing that Jesus's austere instructions were only intended for the rich young ruler, not us, and implying that we can accumulate as much as we want, so long as we don't become too attached to it. This is the core lie that Jesus was putting his finger on, the belief that we can be objective and dispassionate about what we have. *I can have money without trusting in it*, we tell ourselves. But what Jesus wants us to understand, in the strongest terms possible, is that we are lying to ourselves.

For each of us, the question is not *whether* we use money as a form of stability and control, but *how*. And even this can be a difficult question to answer honestly. Thankfully, God has given us a practical solution for examining our hearts, but before we get to it, let's consider one other disordered relationship with money.

Using Money to Control Others

Last year I preached a sermon on Ephesians 5 and marriage, and because the language of "submission" in this passage has sometimes been misused, I wanted to communicate as clearly as I could that I was not endorsing domestic abuse. During the first service, I looked out at our congregation and declared that physical, verbal, and emotional abuse have no place in the kingdom of God. It is the anti-gospel. Marriage is meant to embody the relationship between Jesus and his bride—a relationship in which he laid himself down for her good. Abuse does the opposite. It disfigures and distorts what is meant to be a beautiful witness to God's love.

After the first service, I consulted with a woman from our church who had once endured an abusive marriage and is now a leader and a mentor in our congregation. I asked her if there was anything I should change or adjust in my message, and her advice was so wise. She said, "I appreciate what you said about abuse, because many of us have been trapped in abusive marriages and we needed to hear that truth from the pulpit. But please be sure to include financial abuse in that list. Some women don't realize that the financial control and manipulation they are experiencing is also abuse. And because of that, they will assume what you said does not apply to them."

She was exactly right. In the previous chapter, I discussed Diane Langberg's important book *Redeeming Power*. In it, she outlines the primary types of power that we possess, and I included nearly all of them in that chapter. However, there is one form of power that warrants more focus, and that is **economic power**. Dr. Langberg writes, "Economic power promises and often delivers a certain measure of security and comfort. It can also be used to control, manipulate, and intimidate another person. Money and resources are used as weapons."[3]

An insightful point that Langberg makes about economic power is that it "exposes who we are."[4] Or rather, *how* we use our economic power exposes who we are. If we give "with strings attached," use economic power to constantly protect our kids from the consequences of their decisions, or conversely, give freely and sacrificially for the good of others, we are revealing our true relationship with money.

According to Jesus, we are also revealing our true relationship with him.

The temptation of economic power is to lose our moral bearings. We end up justifying the means with the end, and it happens almost imperceptibly. Just take the example of my negotiating our church's location. One might say I was being shrewd, but I know my true heart. There was idolatry afoot, riding in on the coattails of a godly purpose.

This is why Jesus comes so hard for the love and trust of money. It is why Proverbs condemns it again and again. And it is why the Old Testament prophets single out Israel's neglect of the poor more frequently than almost any other sin. Our relationship with money cannot be passive or vaguely well intentioned. It must be sober-minded, it must be humble, and it must have accountability, and there is one practice that cultivates all three: generosity.

The Narrow Way to Freedom

When it comes to money, Scripture has some perplexing things to say. Proverbs 11:24 is a great example of what I mean: "One gives freely, yet grows all the richer; another withholds what he should give, and only suffers want" (ESV). This is what I like to call "kingdom math." In kingdom math, what is valuable to the world matters little to the kingdom, and what is valuable in the kingdom matters little to the world. In his commentary on the rich young ruler, theologian Stanley Hauerwas summarizes "kingdom math" this way: "Jesus . . . knows well what the rich man lacks. What he lacks is what he has."[5]

What he lacks is what he has. It is a paradox, but it contains a truth we feel deep in our bones. The money in our bank account doesn't *feel* like abundance. That's why Scripture so often describes material wealth as a form of poverty—*spiritual* poverty. It constantly seduces our affections and our trust. It relentlessly vies for our worship with its promises of stability and control, prompting Jesus to warn us in no uncertain terms: "It is easier for a camel to go through the eye of a needle than for a rich person to enter the kingdom of God" (Matt. 19:24 ESV). Of all the alternative "masters" we are tempted to serve in this world, money is among the most enticing.

Does this mean money is, in and of itself, evil? No, it does not. Money is a neutral tool. But as Langberg pointed out, what we do with it exposes and shapes who we are, which is why Jesus instructed the rich, young ruler to give his money away to the poor. Jesus does *not* tell the young man to put his money to good use. He does not say, "Look how God has blessed you! Now go and use it for good!" He simply commands him to give it away, no strings attached. Why? Because **we can use our money for good while still nurturing our craving for control.** This is how truly skilled we are at lying to ourselves. We can avoid reckoning with our control issues by smuggling them in through good works, and

Jesus sees right through this. That's why he tells the rich, young ruler, his own disciples, and us that the only way to be free of this temptation to control is to actively flee from it. And the only way we can flee from it is through radical generosity.

But here is the good news. In the upside-down logic of the kingdom of God, generosity is for others *and* it is for us. It crucifies our idolatry of money, even the deceptive kind that is "used for good." It delivers us from the vain pursuit of wealth's empty promises, and it guards our hearts from hoping in that which betrays. Most importantly, it bears witness to what the love of God is like. Jesus, the Son of God, gave away all the riches and benefits he enjoyed at the right hand of the Father, and it is this extravagant act of love—not his extravagant share of worldly resources—that changes us.

A Prayer of Confession

Jesus, you know me better than I know myself. You know my heart, and you know all the secret idols tucked away in the shadows of my soul. Because you know this, you have warned me—and everyone you love—to be wary of wealth. You know how it swallows up our focus and our dreams. You know how easily we trust in it, instead of you, and you know what this does to our lives. I confess that I have not always believed you—not really—when you have cautioned me about this spiritual peril. I confess that my income has influenced my contentment and that I have sought a sense of control through my finances. Convict me of the vanity of this idolatry and help me to trust you truly.
Amen.

Questions for Self-Examination

1. What sort of relationship with money was modeled for you growing up? How would you describe your relationship with money now?

2. In what area of your life is your contentment or security bound up with your finances?

3. What would "radical generosity" look like in your life now?

6

Autonomy

Everyone did what was right in his own eyes.

Judges 17:6 ESV

One evening Ike and I sat across from a couple who were interested in joining our church. We listened as they described the string of churches they had attended and then left, all within just a few years. They were discouraged and frustrated, but as we listened, we also noticed a pattern. Each time they left a church, it was the pastor's fault. They didn't agree with something the pastor had taught, they didn't like the expectations the pastor had for volunteers, or they received some uninvited feedback from church leadership. And so each time they left.

There are many good reasons to leave a church, and it is of the utmost importance to affirm this. When there is spiritual abuse, narcissistic leadership, false teaching, or a toxic culture, leaving a church is right and wise, and we fully support individuals who come through our doors with these wounds. This couple, however, was describing something different. They had left church after church over nonessential disagreements, and this stood out to us as one more data point in a larger trend we had been noticing.

Historically speaking, the office of pastor or priest has held tremendous authority in local communities. If a pastor said it, then it was nigh close to hearing from God, and in some cultures and churches that is still true. In the United States, however, the authority of the pastor is changing. Increasingly, people will not take a pastor's word for it, and there is good reason for that. Following multiple church and denominational scandals in which the authority of the pastor was used to abuse, it's no wonder Christians and non-Christians are slower to trust.

At the same time, this suspicion of authority is due to a much broader cultural shift we are experiencing, one that has nothing to do with pastors, or the church, at all.

For those of us living in the United States, we are experiencing historically low levels of something called "social trust," a metric that assesses people's belief in the "honesty, integrity and reliability of others."[1] Social trust is nosediving, and we see the effects of this everywhere. For instance, trust in the federal government has plummeted in the last fifty years, dropping from 77 percent in 1967 to roughly 33 percent today. Trust in pastors has seen a similar decline.[2] In 1985, 67 percent of Americans said pastors "had high or very high honesty and ethical standards," but by 2019 that percentage had dropped to 37 percent.[3]

The current decline in trust is not limited to institutional authority either. Americans are also increasingly distrustful of each other. In 2014 the University of Chicago conducted a survey that found only 30.3 percent of Americans agreed that "most people can be trusted," which is the lowest percentage ever recorded since the survey began in 1972.[4]

Because of this shift, Americans have shifted authority away from leaders and experts, instead placing authority in the self. We are taught to trust our instincts because only we know what is right for us and we alone know our truth. Some of this is a

85

healthy, long overdue correction. When we feel unsafe, or when a message sounds shaming, we should pay attention to our intuition and hold these messages up to Scripture, wise friends, or a licensed counselor, instead of simply deferring to whoever is in charge.

But this needed correction can swing into an extreme overcorrection, and we are seeing that in the control we insist on having over *ourselves*. This type of control is not the same as "self-control," which refers to self-regulation, but is more appropriately labeled as "autonomy," which refers to self-governance. Some autonomy is God-given—God was not micromanaging Adam and Eve in the garden, after all—but when it is absolutized, it becomes an unhealthy form of control. This is especially likely to happen when social trust is low. This, combined with the American ideal of individualism, has produced a society that places autonomy as our highest value. New Testament scholar Kavin Rowe describes this cultural value this way:

> The story of the autonomous individual says that the "I" is self-sovereign, emerges into the world without any prior obligations that have been placed upon it, and chooses the laws it has for itself. This story requires us to imagine an isolated individual, unconnected by any necessity to anything else at all, and able to make for itself the life it chooses to make. . . . The territory of the "I" is mine alone—inviolable, sovereign, free.[5]

Rowe warns this is a story we must unlearn because "it is almost impossible for modern Westerners—all of us—not to be caught up by its narrative."[6] I don't think he is overstating this. Each of us has been raised in a "my kingdom" culture whose mantras include "You can't touch this; it's mine," "I make my own decisions, because I know what is best for me," and "No one can tell me what to do." This is fundamentally kingdom language—not "thy will" but "my will be done"—and it is affirmed by our culture of hyper-individualism.

Now, before we get into the pitfalls of this form of control, I want to reiterate that *some* autonomy is healthy and appropriate. From the beginning God imbued us with wisdom to make good decisions. A person with no autonomy whatsoever has been stripped of something God ordained them to have. I also want to be clear that our culture's emphasis on autonomy and its distrust of authority is understandable. History is full of tyrannical leaders who abused their power, but our generation has also witnessed the abuse of authority. Sports organizations like USA Gymnastics or religious institutions like the Roman Catholic Church have undermined public trust in authority, which is why we prize autonomy so highly. It seems much safer to assign authority to ourselves.

That said, when autonomy becomes our guiding moral compass, when we reject any and all accountability in our lives, or when we cast off restraint because we don't like being told what to do, it short-circuits community and stunts our spiritual growth. Case in point: churchgoers who "Amen" their pastor when he rebukes other people's sins, but scoff when the spotlight shines on their own. Whether it is sexual ethics or deeply rooted racism, too many of us would much rather leave than listen.

This is a tension we must reckon with. For too many of us, what we want is not just self-determination but sovereign dominion over self, and this is a problem for two reasons.

We Have Confused Control with Freedom

We live in a culture that equates freedom with not having to do what anyone tells us to do. *I* get to make my own choices. *I* get to live my own truth. *I* get to be who *I* want to be. We call this freedom but it's actually control, and the distinction between the two comes straight from Genesis 3. Adam and Eve enjoyed absolute, perfect freedom, not because they were in charge, but because God was. Unfortunately they made the same mistake we have been making ever since, equating freedom with control. They failed to understand something basic to God's creation, which is that we are at our freest when God alone is on the throne. That is why control—which wants us, not God, on the throne—is diametrically opposed to freedom. Control is just a form of idolatry, and idolatry will never set us free.

Recall Barry Schwartz's book *The Paradox of Choice*. In it, Schwartz gives a really practical example of the benefits of constraining our own autonomy:

> In many ways, social ties actually decrease freedom, choice, and autonomy. Marriage, for example, is a commitment to a particular other person that curtails freedom of choice of sexual and even emotional partners. . . . Most religious institutions call on their members to live their lives in a certain way and to take responsibility for the well-being of their fellow congregants. So, counterintuitive as it may appear, what seems to contribute most to happiness binds us rather than liberates us.[7]

But if freedom is not control over ourselves, what is it? More importantly, how should we understand what freedom is according to Scripture? Once again, the answer can be found in the garden. The freest we ever were was not in the absence of boundaries, but in many ways, within them. When we look back to that fateful moment when Adam and Eve shook off the boundaries given to them by God, we realize that what stole their freedom was not boundaries. What stole their freedom was sin.

This is how Scripture defines freedom: *Freedom from sin.* Freedom to worship God, not self. Freedom to be in right relationship with God, not a slave to idols. That is the ultimate form of freedom, and this understanding is necessary because it reminds us that our freedom does not come from control. Not if true freedom, as Scripture defines it, is being in right relationship with God, unfettered from the brokenness of sin. That is something control cannot give us. Control cannot set us free from sin. Only Jesus can. So the more we follow Jesus and become like him, the freer we will be. *That* is true freedom.

Conversely, if we insist on our own way, refuse to let anyone speak into our lives, and honor Scripture only when it suits us, then our need for control will, ironically, stand between us and true freedom.

We Can Be In Control or We Can Be In Community, but We Can't Be Both

In 1 Corinthians 12, Paul outlines God's vision for the church. He describes a "body" of interdependent parts, of which Christ is the head, and he explains that if a single part of this body is missing, or hurt, then the whole body is affected. This is God's design for the church and his plan for human flourishing.

It stands to reason, then, that we undermine this design when we function as autonomous parts. In fact, this dysfunction happens all the time. For example, when I was single and dating, there were a number of times when wise friends advised me to pull back from a relationship. They could see things I couldn't see. They had perspectives, life experiences, and objectivity that I didn't have. But I would not hear them. To borrow an Old Testament phrase, I did what was right in my own eyes. I proceeded with the relationship anyway, and not only did it end badly and fracture friendships, but it fractured my own sense of self as well. If I had only remembered why God created me as part of a body and that this body was for my protection and my good, I might have been spared a lot of heartache.

Another way we function autonomously is in the rejection of expertise. There are Christian doctors, scientists, journalists, professors, psychologists, and theologians who submit to the authority of Scripture and have devoted their entire lives to pursuing God's truth, but because we live in an autonomous, anti-authority culture, many Christians dismiss professional input entirely and prefer to draw conclusions on their own. This, Scripture warns, is the definition of folly. In the book of Proverbs alone, we are advised again and again to seek wise counsel rather than go our own way:

> Without guidance, a people will fall,
> but with many counselors there is deliverance. (11:14)
>
> Plans fail when there is no counsel,
> but with many advisers they succeed. (15:22)
>
> Victory comes with many counselors. (24:6)

Seeking wise counsel does *not* mean searching the internet for voices that agree with you. It *does* mean seeking counsel from multiple people in your life and in your church who are known to be wise and possess relevant knowledge and experience, because this is God's design. He created us to make decisions and practice discernment in community. It's why he has gifted different members of the body with insight and skill. He has also appointed many of these members to steward their callings with study and training for the health of the body and the common good.

The Anxiety of Autonomy

When we are our own ultimate authority, we undermine the vision of 1 Corinthians 12. Rather than function as an interdependent part of a whole, we function as the head, in place of Christ. In so doing, we become increasingly disconnected from the other members of the body—all of which has consequences.

New York Times columnist David Brooks once wrote an article about the decline in social trust. In his article, Brooks warns of the effect this is having on us as individuals: "Distrustful people try to make themselves invulnerable, [and] armor themselves up in a sour attempt to feel safe." Because of this, they "lose faith in experts. They lose faith in truth, in the flow of information that is the basis of modern society."[8]

When we rely on autonomy to feel in control, we end up distrusting everyone but ourselves, and this produces anxiety. If you can't trust the system, or if you believe no one knows what is best for you but you, then it is all on you to fend for yourself and your family. This is where we get paranoia. This is where we get conspiracy theories. It is the bubbling over of trusting no one and having to scrutinize everything. We think we are the captains of our own destiny, but really, we are alone in a bunker of our own making. It's us against the world.

Thankfully, we don't have to live this way.

In John 14:18, Jesus promises his disciples, "I will not leave you as orphans" (NIV). By this he means he is not leaving them to fend for themselves. Instead, he is sending them an "advocate" (v. 16 NIV) who is the "Spirit of truth" (v. 17). Later in John 16:7, Jesus explains the power of this Spirit when he makes a startling comment. "But very truly I tell you, it is for your good that I am going away. Unless I go away, the Advocate will not come to you" (NIV). Stunningly, Jesus is saying that it is *better* for them—and us!—to have the Holy Spirit than to have Jesus himself in the flesh, because his Spirit indwells us, guides us, and changes us.

And do you know what else the Holy Spirit does? He indwells others too, meaning the presence of the Holy Spirit in others enable us to trust.

If the Holy Spirit is in others, then we can trust the wisdom and counsel of others. Not absolutely, but significantly. Especially since our own sin can keep us from hearing the Holy Spirit correctly. To guard ourselves against self-deception, we need other people who can point out our blind spots, and that is, ultimately, the good news of God's plan for our lives: He has not left us to follow him on our own.

A Prayer of Confession

Gracious God, I confess to you that I love accountability only in theory. Too often, I appreciate accountability abstractly, but not personally. I confess the times I have rejected accountability by becoming defensive, making excuses, or lashing out at the source. I confess to distancing myself from the kind of honest relationships that would challenge and refine me. I confess the belief that I alone know what is best for me.

God, you know all the ways authority is abused, and you do not scrutinize my fear of this. But help me to be honest and repentant when I am withholding trust from trustworthy people—and more importantly, a trustworthy Savior!—because I am only willing to trust myself. And thank you for patiently loving me as I do.

Amen.

Questions for Self-Examination

1. How do you relate to authority? Do you easily trust authority, or do you push back?

2. Whether you trust or distrust authority figures and experts, what led you to this perspective?

3. How does our culture define *freedom*? (There are many answers to this!)

4. Be honest. Are there areas of your life that are off limits to receiving advice?

7

Theology

If anyone teaches false doctrine and does not agree with
the sound teaching of our Lord Jesus Christ and with the
teaching that promotes godliness, he is conceited and
understands nothing, but has an unhealthy interest in
disputes and arguments over words. From these come
envy, quarreling, slander, evil suspicions, and constant
disagreement among people whose minds are depraved
and deprived of the truth, who imagine that godliness is
a way to material gain.

1 Timothy 6:3–5

When Kate Bowler was thirty-five years old, she received a terrifying diagnosis: stage IV colon cancer. At the time, Bowler was a new mom, a professor at Duke Divinity School, and an up-and-coming theologian, all of which accentuated the cruelty of this news. Her pain was then made even worse by people's responses to it. In her memoir *Everything Happens for a Reason: And Other Lies I've Loved*, Bowler recalls the experience of watching people process her sickness and fumble after explanations for why it was happening:

93

"Everything happens for a reason." The only thing worse than saying this is pretending that you know the reason. I've had hundreds of people tell me the reason for my cancer. Because of my sin. Because of my unfaithfulness. Because God is fair. Because God is unfair. Because of my aversion to Brussels sprouts. I mean, no one is short of reasons. So if people tell you this, make sure you are there when they go through the cruelest moments of their lives, and start offering your own. When someone is drowning, the only thing worse than failing to throw them a life preserver is handing them a reason.[1]

Anyone who has ever suffered tragedy knows this pain. The pain of shallow answers. When faced with tragedy, we grope for the right words to make it better, but we end up making it worse. After millennia of human experience on earth, you would think we'd have come up with a more nuanced response than "God has a plan" or "At least you have your health," but when we look at Scripture, we see these responses are bound up in our humanity. It's as if we cannot help ourselves.

Consider Job. Job suffers unthinkable loss due to no fault of his own. He loses his family and all his possessions, and he is distraught. But instead of consoling Job with empathy and care, his friends *blame* him for it with invented accusations: **"Is not your wickedness great? Are not your sins endless?"** (22:5 NIV, emphasis added).

Consider also the man born blind in John 9. We know almost nothing about him and neither do the disciples, but this does not stop them from speculating about the cause of his condition: **"Rabbi, who sinned, this man or his parents, that he was born blind?"** (v. 2 NIV, emphasis added).

Both of these stories are classic examples of "What Not to Do When Your Friend Is Suffering." Of self-awareness or basic human decency, they don't have much! But the million-dollar question is, *Why?* Why was their logic so cruel and inhumane? And why, thousands of years later, are we still doing this?

The reason is actually quite simple. Job's friends and Jesus's disciples responded as insensitively as they did because it wasn't about Job, or the man born blind, at all. It was about them. What they were really doing in each moment was grappling with the reality of suffering in the world. They were scrambling after a narrative that left them feeling safe and protected from unpredictable pain and loss, and that narrative—that this was somebody's *fault*—gave them a sense of control. It is the same reason why, whenever tragedy strikes, onlookers suggest explanations without knowing the details. Whether we blame diet, lifestyle, medical treatments, where a person lives, how a person parents, or the seriousness of a person's faith, all of these answers are a veiled attempt at taming the chaos of the world. Deep down, each of these answers is about control.

They are also theological.

You see, any time you try to explain why bad things happen, you are making a theological claim about God's design for the world. In the examples of Job's friends and Jesus's disciples, they believed that bad things happened to bad people and good things happened to good people, and this "theology" helped them feel more in control. This theology also has a name—the prosperity gospel—and it is this very theology that, ironically, Bowler devoted her doctoral research to understanding.

As Bowler began to process her cancer diagnosis, she discovered how much of this theology was also embedded in her own faith. She writes,

> The prosperity gospel is a theodicy, an explanation for the problem of evil. It is an answer to the questions that take our lives apart: Why do some people get healed and some people don't? Why do some people leap and land on their feet while others tumble all the way down? . . . The prosperity gospel looks at the world as it is and promises a solution. It guarantees that faith will always make a way.[2]

Bowler then concludes,

> I would love to report that what I found in the prosperity gospel
> was something so foreign and terrible to me that I was warned away.
> But what I discovered was both familiar and painfully sweet: the
> promise that I could curate my life, minimize my losses, and stand
> on my successes. And no matter how many times I rolled my eyes
> at the creed's outrageous certainties, I craved them just the same.[3]

When we are sitting in the seat of suffering, or close to it, our
desire for answers is completely human and understandable. Coming to grips with tragedy and loss is difficult, messy work. Yet in
our flailing after predictability and meaning, many of us grab hold
of another form of control in our lives—*theology*. The prosperity
gospel is one of the most popular forms because it is a theology
of control. It gives us a false sense of command over our lives,
and like every form of control we have looked at, it comes at a
cost.

The Lie of the Prosperity Gospel

The prosperity gospel links faith to material prosperity, and it
departs from biblical doctrine in three key ways. First, **it implies
a *contractual* relationship with God**. It teaches that we can receive
God's blessing in exchange for certain acts of obedience. Scripture,
on the other hand, teaches a *covenantal* relationship with God
that stands, first and foremost, on God's faithfulness, not ours.
Scripture says his blessing is made available to us by grace through
faith. It is not something we must earn.

The second difference is **it promises an earthly reward**. According to the prosperity gospel, our reward is not just heavenly, but
worldly. God will grant us financial gain, career success, and the
life we dream of, all in exchange for our faithfulness. In contrast,
the Bible teaches us that Jesus is the reward. He is our prize. And

when Scripture talks about his riches, it is referring to his love, his salvation, his healing, and his life.

The third difference between biblical doctrine and the prosperity gospel is that **it draws a connection between prosperity and virtue**. The prosperity gospel assumes wealth and success are a sign of two things: God's favor, or your goodness. The trouble is, the Bible does not teach this. Instead, it presents a much more complicated narrative. For example, in Psalm 73:3, Asaph writes, "I envied the arrogant; I saw the prosperity of the wicked." In Job 21:7, Job wonders, "Why do the wicked continue to live, growing old and becoming powerful?" And the writer of Ecclesiastes 7:15 observes, "Someone righteous perishes in spite of his righteousness, and someone wicked lives long in spite of his evil."

These verses defy the simplistic worldview of the prosperity gospel, reminding us, instead, that some people are wealthy and successful *because* they are wicked. They have cheated and lied and stolen, and that is why they prosper, not because of their virtue or their faith. In contrast, some people are poor, or struggle financially, not because of a character flaw or laziness, but because of injustice. Much of the Old Testament is actually devoted to this problem. The prophets do not blame the poor for their poverty but, instead, rebuke Israel for its neglect of them.

These three markers help us distinguish the prosperity gospel from the gospel of Jesus Christ, which is especially helpful since the prosperity gospel takes so many different forms. The most well-known form is espoused by televangelist hucksters who promise financial gain in exchange for money, but this theology plays out in more mainstream venues as well.

Several years ago Ike and I attended a conference where a pastor began sharing about his own journey with cancer. He explained that his cancer had gone into remission because he never said the word *cancer* out loud. He argued that our words are powerful and they have the power to bless or curse, so he was not going to speak a curse over his body by using the word cancer. Whenever the doctor would talk about his cancer, the pastor would respond, "That's what *you* say." This is a more common form of prosperity theology, sometimes called "name it, claim it" theology. I will never forget cutting my eyes over to Ike and mouthing the words, "I don't know about this!"

There is also a self-help version of the prosperity gospel. I recently heard a popular author explain how to "manifest" the life you want. Whatever your dreams or goals may be, you can "manifest" them by simply believing them and speaking them into the world. It sounds empowering, but it's really just a lifestyle influencer's spin on prosperity theology.

Wherever we find the prosperity gospel, it is nothing more than a theology that gives us the illusion of control, and like all the other forms of control we have looked at, it does not provide us the outcome it promises.

Why the Prosperity Gospel Doesn't Work

Because the prosperity gospel equates success with effort and/or personal virtue, it implies we have a lot of control over our outcomes: You found your perfect spouse because you were faithful during your singleness. You grew your business because you manifested it. You got the promotion because you worked harder than anyone else. This cause-and-effect relationship is a convenient way to explain our good fortunes, but it has a dark side when we fail. If prosperity is the result of virtue, work ethic, or the strength of our faith, then the *lack* of success must be the result of sin, vice, or a weak faith. We fail because it's our *fault*.

It's an unforgiving narrative, but it's one that we don't mind imposing on others. As I alluded to at the beginning of the chapter, the poor are often blamed for their own poverty. With logic that echoes the disciples in John 9, we place the blame on their character or work ethic without considering where this logic takes us, because it makes the world feel more predictable and fair. Not only is shaming the poor for their misfortune terribly cruel, but this shaming eventually comes back on us. When we don't get into the school we wanted or our job isn't paying the bills or we get a medical diagnosis that upends our lives, it's on *us*.

The sweet promises of the prosperity gospel slap us in the face when we fall down, and this can be especially disorienting and disillusioning for committed Christians who have been faithful their entire lives. When a person grows up in church, follows God, reads their Bible, raises their kids faithfully, and checks every box only to endure terrible suffering and loss, they might feel betrayed by God. Or they might blame themselves. That is what makes the prosperity gospel so unlike the gospel of Jesus Christ. At the point when we most desperately need the comfort of God and his church, the prosperity gospel scolds us and shames us instead.

In addition to blaming us for our failure, both the Christian prosperity gospel and its self-help version exhaust us. Because the prosperity gospel implies we have control, it saddles us with the nagging fear that "I should be doing more." If life isn't turning out the way you planned or your health isn't getting better or your marriage isn't being restored, it's because "you need more faith" or "you need to work harder." If you aren't achieving your goals or finding your spouse or growing your small business quickly enough, it's because "you aren't positive enough" or "you don't really believe in yourself."

This is a crushing weight to bear. This theology sentences its adherents to a life of striving and always wondering if they are good enough. There is no freedom, there is no resting place, and there is no good news in the face of one's own failure. There is only the mocking promise that if you just did a little more, or had a little more faith, *then* it would all work out.

Better News

Prosperity theology is not the only theology we can use to control or to feel in control. Virtually any theology under the sun can be used to rule other people or give ourselves the false sense that we have a monopoly on God's truth. The reason I have singled out prosperity theology in this chapter is that, as Bowler argues, we all have a bit of it in us. All of us, on some level, wrestle with the temptation to earn. This theology exposes itself every time we feel entitled to our successes or judgmental toward those with less. It exposes itself when we feel betrayed by God for the trials we face or when we feel bitter that the wicked prosper. And it exposes itself when we blame ourselves for suffering that is totally beyond our control. On a conscious level, we might be able to look at prosperity theology and reject it as unbiblical. But it's the passing thoughts, the worries that keep us up in the middle of the night, and the throwaway comments that reveal our deepest beliefs.

And so the last thing I want to say to you in this chapter is this: The true gospel is not a rigid contract. Your life is not a constant test. And God is not coming to collect. In Christ we have the assurance of God's unconditional love, of his salvation, of his presence, of his comfort, and of his hope. And there is nothing we can do to undo it.

Nothing.

Not only does the love of Jesus give us rest in a world of striving, but it also reminds us that we can trust him. We don't have to run after false promises of control that will only bite us in the end. God has extended to us a better offer in Jesus, and as simple as it sounds, our primary work is not to earn his protection, but to open our hands and receive it.

A Prayer of Confession

Sovereign Lord, you cannot be played. There are no strings I can pull or buttons I can push to manipulate your will for my life. But I confess that I still try. I confess that sometimes I think I am owed, and I confess to blaming others for their misfortune, because it makes me feel safer and more secure.

Save me from this false theology. Open my eyes to the prosperity theologies I subscribe to in my life, and restore me to the one true gospel that does not give me control but gives me a freedom infinitely better.

Amen.

Questions for Self-Examination

1. In what contexts have you heard or experienced the term "prosperity gospel" before?

2. What forms of the prosperity gospel can you detect in your life?

3. Why is the prosperity gospel so enticing when the gospel of Jesus requires less?

8

Shame

Do not be afraid, for you will not be put to shame;
don't be humiliated, for you will not be disgraced.
For you will forget the shame of your youth.

Isaiah 54:4

My husband's father was an alcoholic and it has taken years for Ike to talk openly about it. It was months after we started dating before he would tell me the reason his father had died. Part of his reticence came from a desire to honor his dad and care for his family, but it was also the result of underestimating the impact his father's illness had had on him as an adult. Frankly, he thought it was behind him. But throughout our marriage, Ike has steadily woken up to the influence his father's actions have had on his life and ministry.

There is a term for adults who grew up with alcoholic parents —adult children of alcoholics—and just this year, Ike learned that a high percentage of ACOAs struggle with codependency. Because children who grow up in alcoholic homes frequently receive the blame for their parent's bad behavior—"You made me do this!" or "I would not have lost my temper if you had behaved!"—this environment shapes kids in a very particular way, communicating the implicit message that they can *control* their parent's mood. Small children, especially, are too young to understand the stages of intoxication and how it affects their parent's behavior, so they assume they, not alcohol, are the cause. If their parent is in a bad mood, the child concludes she must have done something wrong. If the parent is in a good mood, the child presumes she must have done something right. This is the only way a child knows how to make sense of their parent's erratic behavior.

Because of this upbringing, ACOAs develop a very specific illusion of control, which they carry with them into adulthood. As Ike has since explained to me and also written about, ACOAs often believe that if one of their friends or family members is unhappy or upset, it is *their job* to fix it. They are so convinced of their own power to affect someone else's outlook or mood that they easily fall into codependent relationships.

Neither Ike nor I knew this was a common characteristic of ACOAs, or that it was something Ike struggled with personally, until the pandemic started. It is humbling to admit this, but I think we missed it because we don't have a codependent marriage. What the pandemic revealed, however, was that Ike was not codependent with me; he was codependent with our church. He was trying to manage the emotions and anxieties and crises of everyone in our church, which is already an impossible feat, but the pandemic sent him into overdrive until he was burned-out.

Since then, Ike and I have sought more specific counseling for his childhood trauma, and we have learned a lot, all of which brings me to the topic of this chapter. Of all the insights we gleaned from the time we spent with our counselor, one of the most surprising and consequential was coming to understand the connection between control and shame.

Using Shame to Feel in Control

One of the ways victims of trauma and abuse cope with their lack of control is by blaming themselves. The logic goes, "If I did something to cause this, I can do something to keep it from happening again." Even though this logic puts the blame on the victim for what happened to them, the sense of control it provides is worth the shame they feel. The shame purchases a sense of control.

Growing up with an alcoholic parent makes for just such a relationship with shame. At any given moment, an alcoholic parent is warm or cold, affectionate or violent, depending on their level of intoxication. Their mood swings have nothing to do with their child, but the child does not know this. The child incorrectly believes *she* is the one to blame, which fills her with shame but also a sense of control. If she, not her unpredictable parent, is to blame for the bad thing that happened to her, then she can also prevent the abuse from happening again. In this way, shame is the price one pays for a sense of control. If you caused the abuse, then it must mean you can keep it from happening again. This logic provides us with a false sense of agency.

This is the mentality Ike unearthed in himself this past year. The mistaken belief that the abuse he endured was his own fault actually made the world feel less chaotic and capricious, and he carried that illusion into adulthood. The blame and shame of his childhood gave him a false sense of control over others, but it also burdened him with the belief that he was responsible for everyone else's emotions.

For those of you who do not experience shame in this way, this logic may feel counterintuitive, but for some of you who are hearing this for the first time, it is probably an epiphany. That is exactly what it was for me and for Ike. Once we were able to name this subtle function of shame, and identify the false sense of security it provided, it was a game changer for Ike and for our marriage.

104

Using Shame to Control Others

While exchanging shame for the feeling of being in control is a bit counterintuitive, most of us are familiar with the idea of using shame to control other people. Shame is a powerful form of behavior modification, and most of us have experienced it firsthand. As a child, I remember carpooling with a neighbor just as I was recovering from a cold. Although I was feeling better, I still had a lingering sniffle, which my friend's mother could not bear to listen to. After a series of sneezes and sniffles, she yelled from the front seat, "That is DISGUSTING. Sharon, if you sniffle one more time, I am stopping the car!" I was terrified and humiliated. I was a fifth grader with an ordinary cold, but I had been shamed into holding my breath for as much of the ride as I could.

Most of us have had similar experiences to this one, a moment of searing shame that whipped us into conformity or submission. For many women, there was a key moment that reminded us to properly cover up our bodies. For men, shame may have been the motivator for covering up their emotions. Shame can stick with us and shape our behavior for decades, and despite this negative experience—or perhaps because of it—we use shame on others as well.

Nowhere am I more convicted about this form of control than in my parenting. When my kids disobey my instructions or hurt one another, I usually dole out appropriate consequences. But sometimes I completely lose it. I yell. I vent. I corner them emotionally. I once spent an entire car ride with my oldest son, cataloging my disappointment in his behavior, sermonizing about his character, and belaboring my concerns about who he was becoming. He was seven. It was not as if he had shivved another kid in the parking lot. My rant was not only disproportionate to the "crime," but it was in no way, shape, or form helpful. It was a thinly veiled attempt at shaming him into obedience.

Most of us have memories like this from childhood, but we experience this shaming in adulthood as well. On more than one

105

occasion, I have been slapped on the hand (figuratively, not literally) for being too emotional as a leader.

All of these examples—including my parenting rants—are delivered under the veil of righteousness: "I just care about you" or "you are better than this." In truth, when we say these things, we are using shame as a blunt force tool, and that's exactly what it accomplishes. Rather than build up, it bludgeons.

That is the thing about shame: as effective as it seems to be, it is not really effective at all. What it accomplishes is not genuine change, but merely the appearance of it. Again, this is precisely what we see in Genesis 3, when Adam and Eve cover themselves in fig leaves. Shame does not bring people into the light but pushes them deeper into hiding.

One of the most tragic examples of shame's ineffectiveness is the fallout of shaming people into premarital abstinence. While chastity is, without a doubt, God's clear, biblical will for unmarried people, the many shaming approaches to this teaching have completely failed. Rather than cultivate a love for God's Word, shaming only encourages hiding. Case in point, roughly 65 percent of evangelicals have engaged in premarital sex by the age of 22,[1] and nearly half of women who have abortions are churchgoing Christians.[2]

Shame promises control, but it only provides a quick fix, a rushed paint job. What it cannot accomplish is the Holy Spirit transformation that our souls desperately need. It only trains us to be fakers.

The God Who Transforms Us with Love

One of the brilliant things about Scripture is that every inch of its wisdom runs a mile deep. There are no shallows. You cannot plumb its depths. There is always more to discover. So even though we have spent a lot of time in Genesis 3, there is still much more to unpack, especially when it comes to the topic of shame.

Returning to the garden of Eden, I want you to notice that everything falls apart in a very specific order. The serpent deceives Eve, she eats the fruit she has been forbidden from eating, and then her husband eats it too. Then, as soon as sin enters the world, two new afflictions follow on its heels.

Shame and blame.

Shame invades the garden as soon as Adam and Eve realize their nakedness (v. 7). Soon after, they are confronted with their disobedience, but neither is willing to take responsibility for their actions. Instead, they opt for blame. Adam points to Eve (v. 12), Eve points to the serpent (v. 13), and this entire series of events becomes the template for how we process the brokenness of the world. *Shame and blame.*

Keep that in mind.

Now fast-forward thousands of years to the final moments of Jesus's life, where we observe a similar progression. First, Jesus is mocked and humiliated, before being stripped naked and hung on a cross (John 19), an image that directly echoes the nakedness of Adam and Eve. *Shame.*

Then, as Jesus exhales his final breath, he cries out, "My God, my God, why have you forsaken me?" (Matt. 27:46 NIV). In that moment, he experiences the separation and alienation of taking humanity's sin on himself. *Blame.*

Right there, in the middle of Jesus's final moments on earth, is a reenactment of Adam and Eve's final moments in the garden. Shame and blame. Except this time, these events are not transpiring under the limbs of a tree, but under the shadow of a cross.

And that's not all.

Three days later, Jesus is raised to life in another garden, and the first person he appears to is a woman. *A garden. A woman.* Two more signs that Genesis 3 is happening in reverse. But no longer is a garden the backdrop of death; now it is the location of resurrection. And no longer is a woman the entry point of a lie; now she is the entry point of truth. Everything done in the garden is undone in Christ.

For those of us who follow Jesus, this reversal is necessary to recognize and understand. Ever since Adam and Eve first experienced the consequences of sin, humans have been relying on shame and blame to get things done. We shame people into behaving, apologizing, and "doing the right thing." Why? Because we think we can use the tools of the devil to accomplish the will of God.

But in this great undoing, Jesus doesn't look at our shame and blame with the same kind of cynical shrewdness. He does not declare, "I can *use* this! Shame is so *effective* at motivating my disciples!" Oh no. Jesus looked at our shame and our blame, and he nailed them to the cross. In doing so, he definitively denounced the use of shame and blame as "tools for good." They are eternally unfit for the kingdom of God.

Jesus's answer to the shame of sin was not more shame. His answer was sacrificial, unconditional love, and that is still his message today. The next time you feel tempted to use shame—either to control others or to feel in control of yourself—remember that shame is not how our Father speaks to his kids. And the next time you hear the voice of shame in your own ear, remind yourself that shame is not the voice of God, it's the voice of his enemy. God leads and influences us not with condemnation and control, but with love. And thankfully, his love is not like ours.

It is better.

A Prayer of Confession

Jesus, I confess that I sometimes bow to the power of shame. I also confess that I have used shame to change people, including myself.

Thank you that shame is not your way. Thank you for taking my shame and nailing it to the cross so that it would be as far from me as the east is from the west. Thank you for loving me and building me up in your love. Restrain me from using shame to influence myself or others, and deliver me from the false predictability of shame. Help me find perfect security in you.

Amen.

Questions for Self-Examination

1. Can you remember a time as a child when you were shamed into obedience? How did it shape you as an adult?
2. Why do you think shame is so tempting to use, even when we know it isn't Christlike?
3. What has helped you break free from shame?

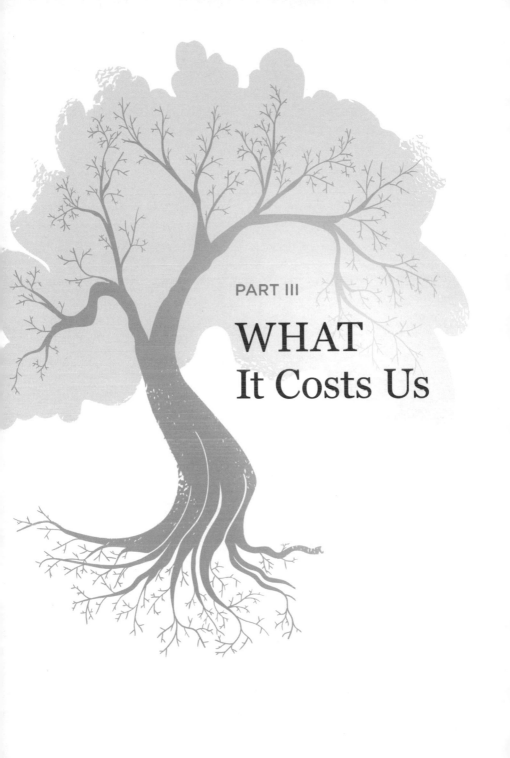

PART III

WHAT
It Costs Us

9

Broken Relationships

The Toxic Impact of
Controlling Other People

One of my favorite shows in the last several years has been
Netflix's series *The Crown*. It is riveting to watch history
unfold, especially while many of the figures featured in the show
are still alive today. The series is somewhat fictionalized, but I
have nevertheless learned a lot about British history and the British monarchy that I didn't know before, including learning about
the mysterious London fog, the deep Christian faith of Queen
Elizabeth, and most intriguing of all, the queen's interference in
the romantic lives of her family members.

Take the story of Queen Elizabeth's sister, Princess Margaret.
At a young age, Margaret wanted to marry Peter Townsend—
an older man who had worked as master of the household—but
Townsend was divorced, which meant a union with Margaret was
expressly forbidden by the Church of England. The British Parlia-
ment opposed the marriage, and Queen Elizabeth found herself
torn between politics and family. In a calculated diplomatic move,

she asked Margaret to wait two years, until her twenty-fifth birthday, when Margaret would no longer need permission from the queen to marry Townsend. Then the prime minister of England got involved. Winston Churchill himself—the same Winston Churchill who fought Hitler and defeated the Nazis!—stepped in to ensure that these two lovebirds remained apart. It is unclear whether he did so under the direct orders of the queen, but he assigned Townsend to the British Embassy in Brussels, which ultimately succeeded in quashing the relationship altogether. After two years had passed, Margaret had abandoned her plan to marry Townsend.[1]

As much as this story takes family meddling to a whole new level, it was not the first, nor would it be the last, time the royal family orchestrated or thwarted matrimonies. Decades after intervening in Margaret's romantic life, the royal family put similar pressure on Queen Elizabeth's son Charles. Following his aunt's example, Charles had his eye on a young woman named Camilla Shand (later, Camilla Parker Bowles), who did not enjoy the queen's approval. Together, the family members and royal aides conspired to shoo Charles away from Camilla and toward an even younger Diana Spencer.

This portion of the Netflix series is especially tragic to watch, because we, as the viewers, know how the story will end. As this young, naïve couple is corralled into marriage, it is clear their relationship never should have been. The consequences of their heavily engineered marriage are devastating and severe: pain, suffering, brokenness, betrayal, and eventually death.[2] It is not an understatement to say that Diana might very well be alive today if she had not become entangled in the British monarchy's marital schemes.

Of course, Queen Elizabeth was doing nothing new. For centuries royal families have relied on marriages to serve as peace treaties. The betrothed were little more than political pawns. At the same time, watching *The Crown* should be a chastening reminder to us all of what can go wrong when we try to control other people.

Thus far in this book, we have looked at the ways we exert control. The *how*. Some of those chapters touched on the relational brokenness that occurs when we coerce or manipulate people with our knowledge, our power, or with shame, but in this chapter, I want to look more directly at the relational cost of control. What we will see in this chapter, and all the chapters to come, is that there is a "law" of control at work: whenever we try to control something in order to fix it, we will end up breaking it even more.

Cost #1: Anxiety

In his book *Managing Leadership Anxiety*, author and pastor Steve Cuss examines the many sources of anxiety facing leaders. He devotes an entire chapter to "Sources of Relational Anxiety," and he explains the many relational dynamics that strain our mental health, chief among them being triangulation. Cuss defines "triangulation" as "any three-person relationship that should have two people in it."[3] Triangulation occurs when there is instability or conflict between two people and a third person is "triangulated" into the relationship in order to deal with, or distract, from the conflict. This often happens to children in divorce. A child is triangulated into the conflict between her parents when one parent vents to the child about the other. Similarly, a father triangulates his family into a conflict with his boss, or his clients, by taking out his stress on them.

Triangulation is not always about control, but Scripture gives us a lot of examples of it being utilized this way. Sarah triangulates Hagar into her marriage with Abraham. Jacob and Rebekah triangulate *against* Esau.[4] There is a double triangulation in the New Testament when Herodias triangulates her daughter, Salome, into her marriage with Herod and then later triangulates her husband into her vendetta against John the Baptist. In all of these situations, a third person is used to neutralize the unhealth or instability of two others.

What does this have to do with control and anxiety? Cuss puts it very succinctly: "Much relational anxiety is generated when we want to change the other, rather than work on ourselves."[5] Triangulation is only one form of control, but it almost always

115

produces anxiety, which is exactly what we see in each of those biblical examples. Using and abusing Hagar did not relieve Sarah's anxiety but made it worse; tricking Esau led to years of family strife and caused Jacob to fear his brother; and despite successfully manipulating her husband via control, Herodias later got them both exiled.

The fact of the matter is we cannot control other people, and whenever we try, it will only produce more anxiety in us. Why? Because, according to Cuss, there are three "spaces" in life that we have some power over but one where we have almost none:

1. The space inside me
2. The space between people
3. The space between me and God
4. **The space inside others**[6]

When we fixate on that fourth space—what is going on inside of others, what their motivations might be, why they act the way they do, or how we can change them—it creates anxiety because we don't actually have control over it. And what the stories of Queen Elizabeth and our biblical characters remind us is that no matter who you are, and no matter how much power you possess, no one is immune to this anxiety. Even some of the harshest, most controlling dictators are hiding a simmering anxiety, because they know, deep down, that they can't really control people's hearts.

Cost #2: Broken Relationships

My middle son, Coen, is constantly breaking his toys. Not on purpose, but by forcing them to bend in directions they were not designed to bend. He has mangled Transformers legs, Avengers figures, and spaceship switches, and he has even cracked LEGOs in half. He pushes and pushes and pushes until *SNAP*. The plastic can't give anymore.

People are like this. When we force them to do something they are unwilling or unable to do, something snaps. It could be their sense of having a voice, their confidence, or it could be the relationship itself that breaks. Relationships and control cannot coexist because God did not design them to. In the garden of Eden, before sin even entered the world, God ruled supreme over creation, but not through control. It was only when Adam and Eve rejected this order, stretching out their fingers for more knowledge and autonomy, that they fractured their relationship with God and with one another.

From that moment on, Genesis describes one relationship after another, all broken by control. Most notable among them is the story of Abraham and Sarah. If you are not familiar with this couple—or you simply need a refresher—Abraham and Sarah are the founding patriarch and matriarch of Israel. After God appoints Abraham to this role, he instructs him to go to a land that God will show him (12:1), and he promises to make Abraham into a great nation. At first Abraham and Sarah trust this promise, obeying God's instructions and walking in faith.

But not for long.

Although God assures Abraham and Sarah of his plan, they begin to make decisions as if God's plan *depends on* them, and this lack of trust manifests in relational control. In Genesis 12, for example, Abraham and Sarah enter Egypt, and Abraham is concerned that he will be killed because of Sarah's beauty, so he tells her to "say you're my sister so it will go well for me because of you, and my life will be spared on your account" (v. 13).

Dutifully, Sarah does exactly what he asks. Soon after, Sarah is invited to the palace, and Pharaoh treats Abraham well on her behalf. He gifts Abraham flocks, herds, and even slaves, which implies this whole charade went on for quite some time.

But like all lies, this one does not remain hidden forever. God strikes Pharaoh and his household with a plague, causing Pharaoh

117

to realize he has been deceived. Once he realizes the scam, he sends Abraham and Sarah on their way.

This whole debacle should have been the end of Abraham and Sarah's attempts to control. It should have taught them their lesson, but it did not. Four chapters later Sarah is still struggling with infertility. Despite God's promise of countless descendants, she cannot get pregnant, and she begins to doubt God once again. I imagine Sarah felt confused, betrayed, and maybe even a little foolish for believing something so impossible in the first place, and it is in this state of desperation that Sarah decides God must need her help. She instructs Abraham to sleep with her slave, Hagar, in order to build a family, and before long the plan seems to be working.

For a little while, anyway.

After some time, it becomes clear that this is nothing more than a Faustian bargain. Not long after Abraham and Hagar's child, Ishmael, is born, Sarah begins to feel jealous of Hagar, and in an act of terrible cruelty, she drives Hagar and Ishmael into the wilderness, vulnerable and alone.

In the quiet aftermath of her actions, Sarah finds herself in the exact same place where she started. Except now she has the abuse of Hagar and the neglect of Ishmael on her hands. She has also unleashed a relational brokenness that will be felt for generations. All because one person thought she knew better than God.

Sadly, the urge to control is a generational sin that repeats itself throughout the book of Genesis:

- Sarah eventually gives birth to Isaac, and then Isaac (like his father before him) tries to pass off his wife as his sister in order to save himself (chap. 26).
- Rebekah—Isaac's wife—manipulates Isaac into blessing her favorite son (chap. 27).
- Laban—Jacob's uncle—tricks Jacob into marrying his oldest daughter (chap. 29).

The stories go on and on. Each new family is fractured by members who trust in their own sovereignty. These individuals connive and deceive and manipulate outcomes, but not once do their actions produce the wholeness they think it will. Never does it bring them closer to one another. Never does it heal or unite. It only breaks and divides.

This is what's at stake whenever we are tempted to control others. It's a reality that genuinely chastens me when I am trying to control my husband. When I am pressing Ike to lead our church a certain way, or make the decision that I think he should make, I now wonder, *What sort of damage is this doing to our marriage long-term?* This truth also haunts me as I raise my kids. They are still young enough that I can "make them" do virtually anything I want, but there is a dance here: balancing my God-given authority as their parent with my limitations as a human being. While I can teach them wisdom and truth and godly habits, I cannot "make them" love activities they do not love or have a specific kind of personality they do not possess. And as much as I wish I could, I cannot make them surrender their lives to Christ. If I try to control these things, I do so at my own peril. To control my children is to undermine my relationship with them in the long run.

That is the second cost of controlling people. Broken relationships are not an *if*, but a *when*. When we try to control people, we will inevitably fracture our relationship with them, because God did not design people to be controlled.

Cost #3: Victimizing the Innocent

This is a brief point, but one worth making. When we look back on the stories of control in Genesis, we can see a pattern:

- When Abraham lies about Sarah, Pharaoh receives a plague.
- When Sarah engineers the birth of Abraham's first child, Hagar and Ishmael are exiled.

- When Isaac lies about Rebekah, he imperils her for his own well-being.
- When Rebekah deceives Isaac, Esau loses his blessing.
- When Laban tricks Jacob, both Jacob and Leah are forced into a loveless marriage.

In each of these scenarios, the person exerting control is spared the brunt of the consequences, while the majority of the fallout is absorbed by those being controlled.

Throughout this book I have asserted that when we use control to fix things, we end up breaking them even more, and this devastation falls disproportionately onto the backs of the innocent. For Christians—who worship a Savior who did not impose his will but instead lowered himself and took the form of a servant in order to protect the most vulnerable of all—this cost of control should especially disturb us.

A Word of Grace

This might be the most difficult chapter in this book, because our desire to control others is not always about arrogance or power. Sometimes it is about love. Sometimes we try to control people because we want what's good for them, which is what makes it so incredibly painful. When your child is being swallowed up by addiction, of course you want to grab them by the collar and snatch them from its jaws. When your friend is about to marry a toxic person, of course you want to do everything in your power to stop them. When your spouse has been unfaithful, of course you want to know where they are every moment of the day. And when your dad has been diagnosed with cancer, of course you want to monitor his diet and doctor's appointments.

In excruciating circumstances like these, our desire for control is understandable and our urgency to act is not wrong. God instilled us with his love, his compassion, and his desire to restore. When we feel those things, and act on them in wise, appropriate ways, we are reflecting our Father in heaven.

At the same time, the hard pill we must swallow—lest we make a bad situation worse—is that our control cannot heal what is broken. You can check your kid into rehab, but you cannot make their sobriety stick. You can counsel your friend not to marry the wrong person, but you cannot stop them from walking down the aisle. You can go to counseling with your spouse, but you cannot guarantee they will not betray you again. And you can dictate everything that your dad puts into his body, but that does not guarantee remission. If we refuse to accept this, we risk pushing people away at the very moment when we need to draw them near.

The health of our relationships, and our souls, depends on our willingness to accept this reality. It is not easy, but I am certain God knew it wouldn't be. Why else would he have come to earth, lived, loved, died, and risen, if not to communicate with blazing clarity that he is a God we can trust? In doing so, he presented us with a choice we must consider every day of our relationship-driven lives: Will I try to control this person, or will I accept that I cannot, and entrust them to God?

A Prayer of Repentance

God of grace, you are not a controlling God. You do not coerce. You do not manipulate. You do not strong-arm. And you do not force. I confess that I have not always imitated your loving gracious influence, but have, at times, tried to control the people I love. I repent of this. Holy Spirit, help me to love and influence those around me according to your character, and restore any relationships that were fractured when I didn't.

Thank you that you do not love the way humans love.
Thank you for pointing us to a better way.
Amen.

Questions for Self-Examination

1. Have you ever felt controlled by another person? How did it affect your relationship with them?

2. Looking back on your life, which people or relationships have you found yourself most tempted to control?

3. What are some of the ways you mask your efforts to control people as "concern"?

4. What were the consequences of trying to control people in your life?

10

Burnout

The Never-Ending Work of Controlling Our Circumstances

In American culture I don't think there is any group more universally picked on than millennials. For well over a decade, millennials have served as the scapegoat of choice for nearly every possible social ill.

Is the economy bad? It's because millennials are spending less!

Is unemployment on the rise? It's because millennials won't get a job!

Housing market on the decline? It's because all those millennials are still living at home!

Are your employees unprofessional at work? Those millennials never learned to adult!

Have raccoons been getting into your trash? It's probably millennials!

If you type "blaming millennials" into your Google search bar, it will complete the phrase with "for everything." Even Google knows!

Now, full disclosure, I am an older millennial (a "geriatric millennial," apparently), and I have learned to tune out most of this criticism. That is, until this year, when I discovered that the generation after me—Gen Z—has *also* begun dumping on millennials. According to the youths, side parts, skinny jeans, and hand-lettered farmhouse wall signs are very over and not cool. Further dumping salt in the wound, my twentysomething baby-sitters have had to put their arm around me and gently explain how to text because, according to them, my texting "sounds angry all the time."

Millennials get criticism both coming and going, and although much of it is silly and fun to laugh about, the trend has had negative consequences as well. In her book *Can't Even: How Millennials Became the Burnout Generation*, author Anne Helen Peterson writes about the uniquely stressful set of circumstances millennials have faced and the toll it has taken on their livelihoods and mental health.

> For millennials, the predominant message of our upbringing was deceptively simple: All roads lead to college, and from there, with more work, we'd find the American Dream, which might not include a picket fence, but certainly had a family, financial security, and something like happiness as a result.[1]

Unfortunately, for many in the millennial generation, this dream has not panned out. In the viral article that inspired her book, Peterson summarized the many obstacles facing millennials today:

> Financially speaking, most of us lag far behind where our parents were when they were our age. We have far less saved, far less equity, far less stability, and far, *far* more student debt. The "greatest generation" had the Depression and the GI Bill; boomers had the golden age of capitalism; Gen-X had deregulation and trickle-down economics. And millennials? We've got venture capital, but we've also got the 2008 financial crisis, the decline of the middle

124

class and the rise of the 1%, and the steady decay of unions and stable, full-time employment.[2]

The combination of the Great Recession and debilitating student debt, along with the astronomical cost of living in urban centers, the increasing cost of childcare, and the soaring price of insurance premiums make millennials "the first generation since the Great Depression where many of us will find ourselves worse off than our parents."[3]

And all of this was true *before* the pandemic.

Of course, previous generations have weathered their own challenges, but Peterson argues that the difference between millennials and other generations—such as "the greatest generation" that fought in World War II—is that the obstacles facing millennials are not fully appreciated. It's as if a chair was thrown under their legs but no one could understand why they tripped.

In reality there is a growing gap between the success promised to millennials if they "work hard enough" and the opportunities actually available to them. This gap is the source of their burnout. Millennials are simultaneously spinning eighteen plates to the point of exhaustion, while being berated for not doing more.

I think Peterson is onto something. In fact, this is one of the only explanations that has helped me make sense of the anxiety in our college students, who are not millennials but are entering adulthood under similar circumstances. I live in the same town where I attended college twenty years ago, and back then the stress was high. My classmates even coined a term for the standard we felt beholden to—"effortless perfection"—so I know a thing or two about pressure. But this is different. The anxiety we are seeing in our students and recent graduates is unlike anything I ever experienced. And if Peterson is right, younger millennials and Gen Zers *are* facing something new: an illusion of opportunity, success, and control over one's future without the conditions necessary to achieve it. They are promised mastery over their destiny if they just "work hard enough," but they are discovering in real time that this promise is a mirage.

All of this brings us to the topic of this chapter: controlling our circumstances. What we see in the millennial generation is the collision of expectations with reality. In a nation that has, for the last several generations, trended upward, our beliefs about the world were profoundly shaped by prosperity. Americans of color have been naming this illusion for centuries, but what we are witnessing now is a universal market correction.

Of course, the desire to control our circumstances—and the inability to do so—is not unique to millennials. We have all been there. We can all think of situations we would like to control and outcomes we would like to engineer, and whether we are able to be honest about it or not, this tug-of-war with reality is a constant source of tension in our lives. Off the top of my head, here are just a few of the things I personally yearn to control right now:

- my children's safety
- my family's financial security
- the health of our church
- racial brokenness in our community
- resources for our local public schools
- the decisions of our government leaders
- our buckling immigration system
- the catastrophic division in our culture and in the church

You probably have your own list. Right now, as you read this, there is probably a situation you desperately wish you could control or an outcome you are frantic to put a stop to. Regardless of our present circumstances, we all feel the temptation to engineer outcomes, and when we do, it costs us in three ways.

Cost #1: More Anxiety

One of my favorite Christmas movies is *Dr. Seuss' How the Grinch Stole Christmas!* In the original animated version, there is a famous scene where the Grinch's heart begins to swell and soften toward Christmas, just as his sleigh of stolen presents is plunging off a cliff. With newfound clarity and conviction, the Grinch scrambles toward the sleigh and grabs on to its runner, attempting to anchor it with his body. Bent like an *L* around the tip of the mountain, the Grinch strains against the weight of the sleigh, but it begins to drag him down. Streams of sweat pour down his face as he manages to hang on, but he is only managing to slow the momentum of the sleigh, rather than stop it. Then, just before the sleigh plummets from the cliff, the Grinch's heart grows three sizes larger, and he gains the strength of "ten Grinches, plus two." He snatches up the sleigh and lifts it over his head like a Seussian Atlas, and in the end the Grinch saves Christmas.

I love this movie and watch it every year, but I also think the image of the Grinch scrambling and sweating and straining and stressing is the perfect depiction of what happens to us emotionally when we try to control our circumstances. When we are smack-dab in the middle of an unpredictable, uncontrollable situation, we stop thinking clearly and our survival mechanism kicks in. Psychologists refer to this as the fight, flight, or freeze response, and when we are in this state, it inhibits our brain's ability to think clearly. All of our body's energy goes toward self-preservation, which is why our urge to control feels so anxious and visceral. Neurologically speaking, control is not a calm, rational response, but a panic-driven one.

Whenever my circumstances feel unpredictable, chaotic, or frightening, I tend to exert control in one of two ways. Sometimes I shift into the gear of "Have you tried this?" I pelt my husband with heaps of "good ideas," and I comb the internet for solutions I haven't thought of. Other times I just get angry. When I feel grief over injustice, I will literally march around my kitchen island, ranting and pounding my fists on the counter. Some of this anger is righteous, but most of it is me wrestling with my total lack of control. I can either take my lack of control to God in prayer or I can go on a kitchen tirade, and I usually choose the latter.

This fear-fueled anger is rampant on social media. Whenever I log online and observe people ranting, trolling, sermonizing, and judging, I often think, *This is about control.* Or rather, the lack thereof. The loudest voices tend to belong to those who feel most powerless. Of course, that is not always a bad thing since social media has provided a much-needed platform for voices that have historically been silenced, but when a person is loud on social media, I tend to assume they feel unheard in real life.

The anxiety we feel when we try to control uncontrollable circumstances manifests in all sorts of ways, but not all of them are public and loud. Some of us live with control-driven anxiety all the time, though at a slightly lower volume. Maybe we aren't constantly online, firing off like a loose cannon, but we are operating out of a chronic, low-grade dread of the uncertain. Whether you are a college student who is about to graduate, you just started a new job, or you just became a parent, these good and normal periods of transition dangle the illusion of control before your eyes, tempting you to forget it's always a devil's deal. It's not just that you cannot control your circumstances, but that you hurt yourself when you try.

Cost #2: Exhaustion

Works righteousness is gonna do what works righteousness is gonna do, and that's what we are really talking about here. The belief that we can engineer the outcome we want is not at all unlike the works righteousness we find in Scripture. If this term is new to you, let me explain it. "Works righteousness" refers to the belief that our standing before God depends on being a good person, living the right way, and doing the right things. It is arguably one of the most common religious beliefs out there, which is ironic because, at its core, works righteousness does not need God. It wants to earn its own way. It wants to be in charge and owe nothing to anyone, even God himself. But what we also see in Scripture is that works righteousness enslaves, because it can never rest.

Control is similar. It trusts in self above all and tells us to rely on our own ability to get things done. It overestimates the value of a good work ethic, as if hard work, or our own sovereignty, guarantees a certain outcome. And like works righteousness, it is founded on an illusion. The trap of works righteousness is that we cannot actually earn righteousness. It is impossible. We are too limited by our own sin. Likewise, we cannot work hard enough to control our circumstances. We are too limited by our humanity. Not only do we lack the power to control our circumstances, but we lack the mental, emotional, and spiritual capacity to keep up. Only God has that infinite bandwidth. He alone can manage the relentless complexity of human circumstances without becoming exhausted by it.

It is for this very reason that God invites us to practice the Sabbath (Exod. 20:8). When we set aside one day each week to rest, we are intentionally acknowledging there is only One who does not need to take a break. There is only One whose oversight is absolutely necessary at every given moment. And it's not you or me.

To declare that God is sovereign is not just a theological statement. It is good news for a weary world. God alone has an infinite capacity to know all things, to manage all things, and to heal all things. When we try to stand in his place by controlling our circumstances, we cast off that protection, trading it in for anxiety and exhaustion instead.

Cost #3: A Powerless Faith

The final cost of controlling our circumstances is one that applies to every area of our lives. I could have incorporated this point in every one of these chapters, especially the previous one on relationships. But I chose to include it in this one since "controlling our circumstances" is a rather broad category.

The truth is, every time we face the urge to control, we are presented with a choice: Will we trust God or ourselves? This question is at the heart of our faith. If faith is believing in what we cannot see, control is the opposite. It is choosing to trust what we can see—namely, our own power, knowledge, and intentions.

That's why control so thoroughly ravages our faith, and it's why our culture of control has left an entire generation of Christians spiritually unprepared to live in the actual world. We are trained, every single day, to trust what we can control and to fear what we cannot see. And it shows.

If we want our faith to grow, and if we want to equip ourselves for discipleship in the real world, then we cannot simply reconcile ourselves to our lack of control; we must *embrace* it. Whenever we are handed the opportunity to trust God's character and will instead of our own, it is also an opportunity to build the spiritual muscle of surrender. And thankfully our days are full of these opportunities.

The Good News

One of the most famous passages in the Bible is Philippians 4:13: "I can do all things through him who strengthens me" (ESV). This verse also appears in a paraphrased form—"I can do all things through Christ"—pretty much everywhere. It appears on marathon T-shirts, coffee mugs, flowery Instagram photos, and farmhouse wall art, inspiring us with its promise of possibility. But because of this pop culture use, its actual meaning has gotten lost.

Philippians 4 is not really about fulfilling our dreams but finding contentment in Christ no matter how difficult the circumstances. In the passage prior to verse 13, Paul writes:

I have learned to be content in whatever circumstances I find my-self. I know how to make do with little, and I know how to make do with a lot. In any and all circumstances I have learned the secret of being content—whether well fed or hungry, whether in abundance or in need. (vv. 11–12)

It is in verse 13 that Paul THEN adds, "I can do all things through him who strengthens me" (ESV). In other words, Paul is able to find contentment no matter what, because *Jesus*, not his circumstances, is the source of his peace.

What this passage achieves that control cannot is a holding together of two contradictory realities. It acknowledges the in-evitable pain and loss of this world, which cannot be avoided, no matter how hard we try. But it also promises that peace and security are always available to us. We don't have to scramble or strive in order to hold everything together, which is good news for millennials and any other human beings who live as if their con-tentment can be achieved. Rather than burn ourselves out pursuing a mirage of satisfaction, we can simply draw near to Jesus, who provides us with something that control never will: rest.

A Prayer of Repentance

Loving Father, you promise to work all things for good for those who love you, which means I do not have to "work all things for good" for myself. And yet, I struggle to trust you in this. I confess that I have engineered outcomes, and I have lived as if my human might was more powerful and necessary for my flourishing than trusting you. I repent of this self-reliance. I repent of striving. I repent of denying my smallness in the world. Thank you that I can trust your plans

even more than my own. But I also ask you, Holy Spirit, to
teach me that trust.
  Amen.

Questions for Self-Examination

1. Did you grow up believing hard work would guarantee you a certain future? Has that matched with your lived experience?

2. As you read through this chapter, did any current circumstance come to mind? What situation do you wish you could control right now?

3. As you reflect on that situation and the outcome you want for it, pay attention to how your body feels. And your mind, your heart rate, your jaw, your shoulders, your breathing. How have you responded?

11

Body Shame

The Impossible Ideal of Controlling Our Bodies

One evening I clicked on a YouTube video and was just about to tap SKIP AD when I was waylaid by a bizarre infomercial. For several minutes I sat transfixed as a British lifestyle influencer modeled a strange beauty product on her face called "anti-aging silicone face patches." I had never heard of these in my life, and I immediately had to find out more.

These silicone face patches are clear and appear to have a rubbery, stretchy texture. You lay them across your forehead, cheeks, and neck—the parts of your face that you want to smooth out—and then you leave them on overnight. If you are wearing all of them at once, you look mildly terrifying—like a futuristic robot who can run your errands and fix your meals but might also murder you in your sleep.

As I viewed testimony after testimony from the product's reviewers, I was both fascinated and confused. I'm no dermatologist, but I assumed this "change" was only temporary—more akin to sitting on a rattan chair that leaves indentations on your leg, not a long-lasting cosmetic fix. And yet each woman crowed about how "good" she looked when she woke up in the morning. "Amazing!" "My neck looks so young!"

To this day, I have not tried silicone face patches (please don't come after me, silicone face patch industry!). But regardless of the results, this beauty treatment is just one example of the many wacky ways we try to resist aging. There is the vampire facial, which involves having your own blood drawn, then applying it to your face. There is bee sting therapy, which is used to treat inflammation and scarring. There are blood-detoxifying leeches, which release an enzyme when they latch on. In 2008 actress Demi Moore described the experience to David Letterman, saying, "You bleed for quite a bit." Then there is snake massage, in which large boa constrictors slither all over your body to help you feel at peace, and presumably, not kill you.[1]

Here's the thing. I personally believe there is nothing wrong with makeup or out-of-the-box beauty treatments, in moderation, if that is what you enjoy. The world is full of weird and wonderful experiences, and our bodies are a form of self-expression. I don't think there is any reason to be legalistic about it.

At the same time, our bodies are ground zero for a lifelong tug-of-war with control, one that we have a hard time even being honest about. Our youth and health contribute to the illusion of control over our bodies, but at the first sign of aging, our culture's beauty industry is ready at the post. The moment our bodies stop submitting to us, there is a plethora of products we can enlist to fight back. In her beautiful book *This Too Shall Last: Finding Grace When Suffering Lingers*, K. J. Ramsey puts it this way:

> The drumbeat of Western culture is that effort produces success. With enough foresight and determination, we each can create life with minimal pain and maximum pleasure. We are proprietors of possibility, the doorkeepers of our own bright futures. Our bodies

are vehicles of productivity, a currency that purchases success or an inconvenience that impedes it.[2]

Because of this "drumbeat," we have been discipled into an illusion of control over our bodies, but Ramsey reminds us that this illusion is not just about vanity. Our desire for youth and beauty—and the lengths we will go to attain them—belong to the broader expectation that our bodies will *serve* us, and if they fail to do so, then we will do everything in our power to *make* them.

This narrative of bodily control is deeply entrenched in each of us because it is marketed to us every single day. There are literally thousands of products and procedures devoted to making our bodies submit to us. Diet supplements and exercise programs control our weight or stave off sickness. Lotions, ointments, and serums reduce the signs of aging. Dye covers our gray hair. Injections soften our wrinkles, plump our lips, and fill our cheeks. Surgeries conform our bodies to the culturally accepted standard of beauty, or even one's preferred gender. But the scope of our seeming control does not stop there.

The relationship between control and our bodies gets very blurry around medical care. On the one hand, medical treatment can itself be a form of control. When doctors are unable to give us the results we want, we might feel betrayed by them, as if medical experts and modern medicine have godlike powers to heal. On the other hand, some people control their bodies by *rejecting* modern medicine. The Christian Science religion, for example, rejects most forms of medical care and instead relies on prayer.

This is complicated stuff, which makes it difficult to speak helpfully about it. When are we controlling our bodies, and when are we simply being wise? When are we expecting too much of our bodies, and when are we strenghtening them? And in all of this, what is Truth with a capital *T*, and what is just our opinion?

135

What Controlling Our Bodies Is Really About

Before we can answer these questions, let's look to the question *under* the question, the core motivation behind our desire to control our bodies. Because until we answer this question, we will only be treating the symptoms, rather than the cause:

What makes our bodies good?

If you pull back all the layers of controlling our bodies, you will find this question at the center. When we do not know how to answer this question correctly or biblically, we rely on control to *make* our bodies good. And not surprisingly, this temptation is very old.

Once again, we find ourselves in Genesis 3. When sin first entered the world, one of the immediate consequences of Adam's and Eve's disobedience was that their relationship with their bodies was broken. In his book *Disability and the Church: A Vision for Diversity and Inclusion*, author Lamar Hardwick explains, "Humanity has had a longstanding challenge with how we view our bodies. Like Adam and Eve, we all have an adversarial view of our bodies that God never intended for us to have. It is a consequence of the fall."[3]

This "adversarial" relationship is the key that unlocks what happened with our bodies at the fall, and this is a detail I absolutely do not want you to miss. Adam's and Eve's bodies were affected by the fall, and we know this, because God tells them so a few verses later. But the first sign of brokenness was not sickness or physical pain, but **their broken relationship with their bodies**. To the human eye, nothing had changed. Theologically speaking, their bodies were still "good." But they no longer recognized them as such, and this is the root of our controlling relationship with our bodies: we believe our bodies are not good, so we try to make them good.

136

All of this raises the next logical question, which is *how* are we defining good? What standard have we set for our bodies in the first place?

To answer this question, I want to present you with two definitions of "good." The definition the world has provided, which is probably most ingrained in us, and the definition given to us by God.

WHAT MAKES A BODY "GOOD"?

THE WORLD'S DEFINITION	GOD'S DEFINITION
• YOUTHFUL	• MADE BY GOD
• THIN	• REFLECTS GOD'S IMAGE
• IN SHAPE	• IS GOD'S CHOSEN TEMPLE TO HOUSE HIS HOLY SPIRIT
• "BEAUTIFUL" OR ATTRACTIVE	
• NOT SICK	
• NOT LIMITED BY DISABILITY	
• ALWAYS FEELS GOOD	

When we look at these two definitions side by side, we see one glaring problem: the world's definition of "good" does not apply to everyone. When we subscribe to the world's definition, our bodies become progressively "less good" as we age. And because this definition is about what our bodies can *do*, it diminishes the image of God in those with disabilities.

In contrast with the world's definition, God declares our bodies to be good by virtue of the fact that he created them, that they bear his image, and that nothing can take this inherent goodness away. This theology becomes the baseline for how we relate to our bodies. For example, in 1 Corinthians 6:19–20, Paul writes, "Don't you know that your body is a temple of the Holy Spirit who is in you, whom you have from God? You are not your own, for you were bought at a price. So glorify God with your body." Here Paul is urging the Corinthians to honor and care for their

137

bodies, not for the sake of making them good, but *because they already are good*. This motivation helps us discern the difference between care and control. As Jess Connolly puts it in her powerful book *Breaking Free of Body Shame: Dare to Reclaim What God Has Named Good*, whenever we exercise or go to the doctor or eat enough nutrients in a day, we need to ask ourselves: **Am I trying to make my body good, or am I simply taking care of what God has already called good?**[4]

But what about disabilities or chronic illness? When we take advantage of medical experts or state-of-the-art therapies to improve our quality of living because we are sick or growing older, are we "controlling" our bodies? Are we forcing them to submit to our wills instead of surrendering them to God? Are we refusing to accept the goodness of our bodies as they are?

I don't think so. God has given us brilliant scientists and doctors who have developed technology that can heal, and this, too, is a sign of his kingdom. Healing in all its forms emanates from the Great Physician, and it is a foretaste of what awaits us in eternity. Making that distinction between medicine as control versus medicine as a gift is what matters, but also know this: even if you do struggle with wanting to fix your body because you are exhausted and demoralized and tired of living in pain, your heavenly Father understands. He is not standing over you, wondering why your relationship with your body isn't better or why you can't simply trust him more. For over thirty years God lived on earth in human flesh, and when faced with the physical agony of his impending crucifixion, he asked if there was any way out of it (Matt. 26:39). Yes, he ultimately submitted to the Father, but that moment of naked humanity reminds us that trusting God with our bodies is not a pass-fail test. We will all struggle with our bodies, and there will be days—years!—when they do not feel good at all and we wish we could improve them or make them more whole. God does not judge us for this. He has literally been there so that we don't have to stay there alone.

The Cost of Controlling Our Bodies

Bearing this grace and nuance in mind, let's consider what is at stake when we make the choice to control our bodies and squeeze them into the world's definition of "good." What is the cost? There are two primary consequences I want you to consider, but before I explain what they are, I am going to share two stories about the ways we inadvertently harm ourselves when we try to control our bodies. Since both touch on sensitive topics, I wanted to give you a heads-up. The first story is about childbirth and the second about disordered eating.

When I was pregnant with our first son, Isaac, Ike and I took a class on natural childbirth. We enrolled in the class, not because of our personal convictions about medical intervention, but because we wanted to learn as much as possible about the labor and delivery process. We thought this class would equip us, and it certainly did.

What I appreciated most was how thoroughly the class prepared us for the birthing experience. We learned about all the options available to us and what questions to ask. Then, at the end, we made a birth plan that we printed out and shared with our doctor. By that point I felt capable and equipped, and if I'm being really honest, I also felt in control.

Eleven days after my due date had come and gone, I finally went into labor, and it didn't take long before my birth plan went out the window. Not only was I in labor for well over twenty-four hours, but I also developed rapid onset preeclampsia in the middle of it. Preeclampsia, if left untreated, can lead to fatal complications for both the mother and the child, so I was given a treatment of magnesium to keep me safe and an epidural to help me rest. Not long after the epidural, I delivered Isaac.

Several months later, our class regathered to meet one another's babies. It was magical to see all the little people we had been preparing for together. Many of the women had delivered exactly as they had planned, and they had beautiful stories of endurance and strength. But some of the women in our class—like me—had very different experiences. We had gone into the experience with a sense of control over our bodies but came out greatly humbled. I will always remember talking to another woman who had been zealous to deliver naturally. She swore she would never accept medical intervention, and she succeeded in achieving that goal, but the delivery was not at all what she expected. She experienced numerous complications that caused her labor to be so exceptionally long and excruciatingly painful that she doubted she could ever go through it again.

Not every mother has the experience that I, or my classmate, had. But for me, labor and delivery was a wake-up call. It was the first time I realized the frailty of my body. It was also the first time I was confronted with my own mortality. As wonderful as the birthing class had been, as much as it taught me how to advocate for myself, and as grateful as I was for all that I learned, I interpreted my newly acquired knowledge in a distorted way. While my body *is* strong and powerful, and giving birth *is* miraculous, I will never again mistake these things for control.

Like many wives, one of the things I used to be secretly jealous of my husband about is his ability to gain or lose weight on command. If he wants to gain muscle mass, he knows exactly how to do it. If he wants to lose weight, he knows exactly how to cut it. Some of this is due to his body type and metabolism, but some of this is a holdover from his days as a wrestler.

When Ike was in high school, he was the captain of his wrestling team, and one expectation that he and every one of his teammates were beholden to was "making weight." Prior to every match, each wrestler had to make weight in order to qualify for their weight class. The goal was to manipulate their weight so that they were at the top of their weight class without tipping into the one above it. This gave them a competitive advantage, but it also meant that, during wrestling season, their lives revolved entirely around diet, exercise, and how much they weighed. If they needed to pack on some weight, they would eat more and build more muscle. But if they weighed too much on the day of the match, they would engage in dangerous weight-shedding behaviors. Ike once told me he went running in eighty-degree weather, wearing a sweatshirt, sweatpants, and a garbage bag in order to sweat off the weight.

These young athletes seemed to have a remarkable amount of control over their bodies. They knew exactly how to gain or lose the weight they needed. And yet, I wonder how many of them still have an unhealthy relationship with their bodies, or with food, because they wrestled in high school or college. As disciplined as wrestlers have to be about their weight, and as much as it would appear that they used to reign sovereign over their bodies, these habits affected them both physically and psychologically. A recent study found that nearly half of wrestlers are at risk of developing an eating disorder, and in some very rare cases, students who engaged in extreme weight cutting died.

In both of these stories, the illusion of control looms large. In fact, both demonstrate why the illusion is so enduring—sometimes it works. Sometimes women make birth plans that go exactly as they imagined. Sometimes wrestlers are able to manipulate their weight without any long-term damage to their bodies or their minds. It works just well enough, just often enough, to prop up the illusion that we have more control than we actually do, which is why so many of us fall prey to the myth that, with the right tools or the right training, we can subdue our bodies.

But it's a lie. Like all the other forms of control, it's a devil's deal. And in the case of our bodies, the net result is an exact reversal of the control we seek, which leads us to the first cost of control.

Cost #1: When We Try to Control Our Bodies, They End Up Controlling Us

Anyone who has struggled with disordered eating has experienced this Faustian bargain personally. Whether or not the habit begins as a form of control, it quickly devolves into bondage. The object of our control ends up controlling us instead, and this plays out in all sorts of ways besides diet. Returning to my own story of giving birth, I have had many friends feel bound to deliver naturally, or to breastfeed a certain length of time, only to have this expectation stand over them, demanding more, even after they reached their physical limits.

The same reversal happens with beauty products and procedures. We may begin wearing makeup or getting small procedures done because we enjoy it, but sometimes that wanting and enjoying shifts to *needing*. Anytime our joy or contentment *depends* on our body's conformity to a standard, or ability to perform, then it is our body—not Christ—that determines our contentment and joy.

Some of the clearest, most prophetic voices on this subject are people with disabilities. In *Suffer Strong: How to Survive Anything by Redefining Everything*, coauthor Katherine Wolf writes about the lessons she learned from having suffered a stroke that paralyzed half of her face and left her unable to walk. In her book, she explains the realization that

> We are all disabled. None of us have unlimited access to whatever we want or whatever we planned for our lives to look like. We are

142

constrained by our marriages or our singleness, by our children or our childlessness, by our obligations or our debts, by obstacles real or imagined. No one enters life or leaves it without feeling bound by something.[5]

Wolf is repeating a common refrain in disability theology, which is that limitations are a part of being human. The perfect human is not one without limitations, and the reason we know this is because Jesus himself was limited. He needed food, water, and rest. He experienced suffering and pain, and none of this detracted from his perfect humanity.

What does this mean for us and our everyday lives? It means that our standard of good and our prerequisite for joy must not be a body without limitations. If we cannot have contentment without the absence of limitations, then we will never be content. Life will inevitably weaken our physical capacity in one way or another, which is why our joy cannot depend on "fixing" our bodies, whatever "fixing" means to each of us. While it is good to take care of our bodies, love our bodies, and glorify God with our bodies, our satisfaction cannot depend on our ability to control them. As long as it does, our bodies will control our joy and contentment in life, which means they will also control us.

Cost #2: Controlling Our Bodies Will Make an Enemy of Them

Here is a hard but undeniable truth: you will not win the battle against aging. None of us will. Whether the struggle with your body has been lifelong or it is just now emerging, time will only accelerate your body's rapid retreat from all that the world calls beautiful, valuable, and good. I know that sounds bleak, but for those of us who are in Christ, whose eternities are sealed in his resurrection, it needn't be. "To live is Christ and to die is gain" (Phil. 1:21), and that is great news! Truly! Every passing day brings us closer and closer to our resurrected bodies. And more importantly, to the One who was resurrected.

Some of us, however, are not living with this hope. When our physical beauty begins to fade or our health declines, it's as though our bodies have betrayed us. They have failed to live up to some unwritten bargain, and because of this, we resent them.

Entire books have been written about this struggle, so I will not attempt to cover all that is entailed in that conversation. Instead, I will commend to you authors like K. J. Ramsey, Lamar Hardwick, Jess Connolly, Katherine Wolf, Joni Eareckson Tada, Alia Joy, Kate Bowler, and the many others who have not only lived this ache but spoken the gospel into it.

Good News for Broken Bodies

I want to close this chapter rather simply. In each of these chapters about the cost of control, I have wanted to leave you with good news. While the enemy offers us a devil's deal, God offers us something infinitely better: himself. In Jesus Christ, we have a better, sturdier hope than the fleeting, empty promises of control. This hope is for our souls, but it is for our bodies also, all because God became human.

That is the good news for our bodies. Jesus took on flesh—a *body*—to reconcile us to our own. The broken relationship we have with our bodies, which was present from the moment sin entered the world, will one day be reversed because of Christ. So, wherever you find yourself in relationship to your body, just know this: as much as you think about, agonize over, work out, diet, and push your body, there is still no one more committed to its healing and wholeness than the One who created it in the first place.

A Prayer of Repentance

God who came near, you know what it is like to live with a body. You loved me enough to come to earth and teach me how to honor my body as you intended. But I confess this is hard. I confess to resenting my body when it does not co-operate. I confess to dishonoring my body with how I speak about it or think about it. And I repent of mistreating my body, degrading my body, and belittling my body. Comfort me as my body feels the effects of living in a broken world, but also restore my relationship with my body's goodness, for my freedom and your glory.
Amen.

Questions for Self-Examination

1. How would you describe your relationship with your body right now?
2. What characteristics of your body, if any, seem "good" to you?
3. In what specific ways have you tried to control your body (diet, exercise, health supplements, performance, etc.)? Did you experience any of the costs detailed in this chapter as a result of those decisions?
4. How can you tell the difference between caring for your body because it is good and controlling your body to make it good?

12

Anxiety

The Balancing Act of Controlling
Our Reputations

When I first met Ike, his dad had died only five months before, and it was complicated.

Ike's parents had divorced several years prior to his father's
death, but his mom still held some hope of reconciliation. She
loved Ike's dad to his dying day, but he was an alcoholic, and that
was ultimately the reason they separated. Deep down she dreamed
that, if he ever got sober, they might one day find their way back
to one another, but that dream died along with him.

Over the years I have listened to my mother-in-law process the
many layers of her grief, and one part of her story has profoundly
shaped me. In the aftermath of the divorce, there were different
narratives about who was to blame because divorce is rarely one-
sided. At the same time, not everyone knew about my father-in-
law's addiction, which was a significant part of the story. Without
that information, many of their mutual friends—including parts
of their church community—knew only a piece of the story, but

my mother-in-law felt that going around and telling her "side" was not the way to go.

This half story impacted her reputation, a fact that hung over her like a cloud for years. When Ike and I were dating and I was first getting to know her, the pain of having her reputation in doubt was at its freshest. She wanted to sit down and explain it to people, but she also knew she could not. The truth of her character had been submerged deep under the waters of hearsay, so she had to wait and trust that it would, over time, rise back to the surface.

Thankfully, that is exactly what happened. As time passed, and the fog of the divorce lifted, she began to experience restoration in relationships that had been broken. In fact, that is one of the most beautiful things about our extended Miller family. They have re-embraced my mother-in-law over the years, inviting her to every family reunion and welcoming her with open arms. It is truly remarkable. Likewise, any friendships that were affected by the divorce have mostly been repaired. After years of alienation and feeling totally helpless, my mother-in-law's patience paid off.

I tell people this story all the time. To me, it is a powerful testimony about the power of character to shine through. Whether one's character is corrupt or deeply formed by Christ, the truth will make itself known in time.

But boy is it hard to trust this principle in the interim, which is why many of us struggle to do so. It is painful to have our names dragged through the mud, so the tendency to control what people think of us is understandable. But when we do, we can expect two primary costs.

Cost #1: Still More Anxiety

This area of control is closely related to the chapter on controlling other people, so the costs are similar. Recall Steve Cuss's explanation of the four "spaces" around us and the one space over which we have the least influence:

1. The space inside me
2. The space between people
3. The space between me and God
4. **The space inside others**[1]

When we try to control our reputations, what we are really doing is trying to control what people *think* of us, and this not only leaves us guessing about what they think, but probably assuming the worst:

> If my kid shows up to church dressed like that, *what will people think?*
>
> If my husband and I go to a marriage counselor, *what will people think?*
>
> If I drop out of my graduate program, *what will people think?*
>
> If I quit my job to stay at home, *what will people think?*
>
> If I leave this abusive relationship, *what will people think?*
>
> If I stand up for a cause that is biblical but controversial, *what will people think?*
>
> If I share openly and honestly about my past, *what will people think?*
>
> If I confess my present struggle with sin, *what will people think?*

Whenever we find ourselves asking this question, we are unlikely to fill in the blank optimistically. In our imaginations, the answer to "What will people think about my divorce?" is not "They will probably give me the benefit of the doubt and support me with compassion and grace!" Oh no. Whenever we are engaged in this sort of "mind reading," we almost always assume the worst, which is one of the many reasons why this question makes for a terrible compass. When we are guided by the question "What will people think?" we are likely to make decisions based on anxiety.

Cost #2: Moral Corruption

Another result of controlling our reputations is that we become intentionally deceptive. We will show up to church, put on the facade of a "nice Christian," and never be honest about our private lives. That is what we do when reputation is our god. Honesty gets sacrificed on its altar.

This hypocritical faith is bad for our souls and leaves us spiritually disjointed, but its consequences turn sinister when we are talking about the reputation of an *institution*. Whenever an institution's reputation is at stake, all sorts of corruption get locked away in a closet—sexual abuse, bullying, infidelity, cheating—all for the sake of protecting the "good" that the church or business or athletic program has done. The fallout is catastrophic, which is why I wrote an entire chapter on controlling our reputations. Controlling what people think of us is about so much more than people-pleasing. When it is not enough to *be* good, and we want people to also *think* we are good, then we are likely to protect our reputations in destructive ways.

Proverbs 22:1 says, "A good name is to be chosen over great wealth," but when we protect our reputations at all costs, we are not talking about protecting a "good name." We are talking about protecting an idol. And do you know what idols don't accept? Accountability. We can always tell idolatry is afoot when preserving our reputation is more important than holding ourselves to an ethical or biblical standard.

The cost of controlling our reputations is high—for our mental health and for our integrity. When we refuse to swallow the pill that, sometimes, people will not like us or think well of us, or when we cannot accept the fact that it is actually better to tell the truth than a lie, the consequences are much, much worse. This hypocrisy

149

WHAT It Costs Us

produces anxiety, inauthenticity, cover-ups, and ultimately, spiritual death, because we are cultivating a false exterior while our souls wither beneath it.

Living for a Higher Cause

One reason I have clung to my mother-in-law's story so tightly is that this particular form of control is very hard for me. When I stepped into church leadership, I was not fully prepared for the ways my name would be thrown around so recklessly. I have felt sucker punched by the casual gossip that has even come from the mouths of my friends. Most of it I can shake off, but the one thing that really keeps me up at night is the accusation of being unbiblical or lacking a sufficient focus on Jesus. If you want to knock me off my feet, you can hit me with that.

When this happens, I go into mind reading mode. I guess at what people are thinking, and I argue with them in my head for hours. I have spent entire days doing this—mounting my case, correcting their errors, and most importantly, restoring my reputation. *How dare THEY say I am not being biblical. I am the MOST biblical!* Then I fantasize about what would happen if I could only say these things in person.

What I am *actually* doing when I go down this mental spiral is torturing myself. And do you know something I really hate doing? Torturing myself. As it turns out, all this daydreaming about dunking on people only makes me more miserable, not less. That's why, over time, I realized I needed to make a decision: I could either anguish over my reputation or I could release my reputation to God and sleep better at night.

Of the two options, I liked the second one better. The second one also sounded a lot more like the gospel. But again, the question is, *How?* How do we cultivate God-honoring reputations without holding on to them too tightly? When I look at Scripture, I see two answers.

Trust Your Character to Speak for You

Did you know that besides Jesus there is only one other person in the Bible who is never described as having sinned? Joseph in Genesis. We have no recorded documentation of his sin. Of course, he did actually sin, because he was human, but the Bible simply doesn't tell us about it. What we do know about Joseph is that he was a man of integrity, patience, and unwavering faithfulness. Joseph passed every test of his character and trusted God no matter what. Even more amazingly, he remained soft-hearted through all his trials and temptations. He won people's affections, he was trustworthy, and he forgave. He was the kind of person, and leader, that any one of us would want to emulate.

Despite all this, he was not universally liked.

First there are his brothers. Joseph is his father's favorite son, because he has been born to him in his old age. His father loves him so much, in fact, that he makes him an ornate robe, as if to rub it in his other sons' faces. Not surprisingly, Joseph's brothers hate him for it. They begrudge him so deeply that they refuse to even speak a kind word to him.

But then come the dreams. Joseph begins to have dreams in which all of his brothers bow down to him, and Joseph's response is perhaps the clearest sign of his humanity. In an act of painstaking naiveté, this most-favored son, who is already disliked by his brothers, decides to tell them about his dreams. *Twice.* Some interpreters assume Joseph does this out of pride, but the truth is we don't really know. Perhaps he simply wants them to share in his excitement, but unsurprisingly, they do not. The dreams only fuel his brothers' rage even more.

Their jealousy boils to the surface one day when they are out tending their father's flocks. Far away from the prying eyes of any witnesses, they seize Joseph, strip him of his coat, sell him into slavery, and tell their father that he died. Not because of anything Joseph had done to them, but because of their own craven envy.

Then there is Potiphar's wife. After being sold into slavery by his brothers, Joseph lands in Egypt where he works for one of Pharaoh's officials, a captain named Potiphar. Joseph quickly finds favor, and it isn't long before Potiphar trusts him implicitly and puts him in charge of his household.

Meanwhile, Potiphar's wife takes notice of Joseph too. Genesis 39 tells us that Joseph was handsome and well built, so she invites him to bed multiple times, and each time he refuses. In her bitterness at being rejected, Potiphar's wife goes to her husband and falsely accuses Joseph of trying to rape her. Feeling both betrayed and enraged, Potiphar throws Joseph into prison, and once again his reputation and his future seem to be ruined, due to no actual fault of his own.

Joseph was, by all accounts, a good and decent man. He was dependable and loyal and had a strong sense of right and wrong. And yet, his good name was dragged through the mud on more than one occasion, which means his integrity did not protect his reputation.

But what we see in the grand arc of his life—as well as my mother-in-law's—is that character is undeniable. The Greek philosopher Heraclitus once said that "character is destiny," and Scripture affirms this again and again. It is, in essence, what the entire book of Proverbs is about. While we cannot control what other people think about us, the manner in which we live is what ultimately sets our course.

Any time we find ourselves the subject of rumors and gossip, this truth *must* be our steadying hope. So much is at stake when it is not. We must trust that our character, and the character of anyone who slanders us, will eventually be revealed, because taking matters into our own hands never works the way we think it will.

The good news is that character is *loud*. Bad character and good. If given enough time, it eventually shines through, and that truth brings me a lot of comfort. I cannot control what other people think of me, but I can cultivate a godly character, and that character will speak for itself.

Your Reputation Doesn't Ultimately Matter

As I am writing this, there are three different people in my and Ike's lives who are upset with us. Standing in the kitchen this afternoon, Ike looked at me somewhat bewildered and said, "I have never had so many people mad at me at once for not doing anything!" What a time to be alive!

In each of these situations, I want to defend myself. I don't want them to think poorly of me or Ike or our church, and the more I ruminate on this, the more anxiety I feel. As I drove to pick up my sons from school, I stared out the window, lost in thought about it all, when the Holy Spirit disrupted my spiral with this good and holy reminder:

It's not about you. You aren't doing this for you.

Instantly I breathed a sigh of relief. My shoulders released the tension they'd been bearing. My jaw unclenched. *Yes. YES. That's right. That's why I am doing this. Not to win people to myself, but to win them to Jesus. My reputation isn't getting anyone to heaven.*

No one embodies this freedom more contagiously than the apostle Paul. I have already mentioned Paul's famous words in Philippians 4, but the verse that has impacted my life far more than that one comes from Philippians 1. In this letter, which he wrote while under house arrest and facing an uncertain future, Paul describes the moment of realizing that some Christians are rejoicing in his imprisonment. They consider it an advantage for their own ministries, and rather than despair at the hideous betrayal of these so-called brothers in Christ, Paul responds with an astonishing lightness: "What does it matter? Only that in every way, whether from false motives or true, Christ is proclaimed, and in this I rejoice" (v. 18). It makes no sense that this is his response. After all, these men should have been proud of Paul and his commitment to the gospel of Jesus Christ, but instead they heaped betrayal on top of an already bleak imprisonment. If it had been me, my bitterness would have known no end! But not Paul. His reputation, his success, and even his life mattered less to him than the mission of preaching Christ, no matter the lips preaching it. And that, right there, is the key to freedom.

We cannot be free if we do not hold our reputations lightly. Does this mean our reputations mean nothing? Of course not. In 2 Corinthians 3, Paul refers to us as "Christ's letter" of recommendation, "not written with ink but with the Spirit of the living God" (v. 3). We are Jesus's representatives on earth, which means our lives matter. Our integrity matters. Our truthfulness and humility matter. Each time the church earns a bad reputation because it has abused power or been complicit in sin, another unnecessary obstacle is added between people and God.

So yes, we must guard our reputations with the quality of our character, and we ought to correct people when they have been misinformed. But we must never mistake who we are winning people to. We are not winning people to ourselves, and we are certainly not winning them to our reputations. We are winning them to Jesus, and Jesus doesn't need our reputations to be perfect for his gospel to spread. In fact, we wouldn't have needed him in the first place if that was the case.

So let it go. Let people think what they want. We cannot save them, so let's focus on pointing them to the One who can.

A Prayer of Repentance

Thank you, Jesus, that there are no skeletons in your closet. Your character is perfect. I do not have to worry about discovering any deep dark secrets in your story, because you are exactly who you say you are: life. You are salvation for all

who come to you, which is why, ultimately, it is only your name that matters. It is only your name that saves. Not mine. I release the idolatry of my own reputation and recommit to pointing others to you, because living for your name alone is freedom.
   Amen.

1. How do you think people would describe you? How do you *want* people to describe you?
2. Can you think of a time when you talked about someone behind their back in an unflattering way? Why did you do it?
3. When you find out someone has done the same to you, how do you tend to respond?
4. In your mind, what is the difference between guarding your reputation and controlling your reputation?

13

Exhaustion

The Surprising Striving of Controlling Our Identities

I have a boy and two girls—until they tell me otherwise."[1] One afternoon I was listening to an interview with bestselling author Glennon Doyle when she made this comment in passing. Doyle was describing her unconditional support for her children, no matter the path they choose—whether that be vocationally, sexually, or regarding their gender identity—but as she moved on to a different topic, my mind lingered on what she had just said.

This is exactly how our culture thinks about identity. Within a generation, we have witnessed a dramatic shift in Western culture's understanding of identity. Not too long ago, identity was considered to be somewhat fixed, but now it is much more free-form. The process of finding one's true self is a combination of uncovering your authentic "you" and being whoever you want to be.

What is fascinating about this shift is how it dovetails with our culture's already overwhelming number of choices. In *The Paradox of Choice*, this is one of the more surprising sources of overwhelm that Schwartz describes. Whenever we have endless opportunities and limitless freedom, we become bogged down by the options, and this includes identity. Schwartz writes,

> Each person comes into the world with baggage from his ancestral past—race, ethnicity, nationality, religion, social and economic class. All this baggage tells the world a lot about who we are. Or, at least, it used to. . . . Now greater possibilities exist for transcending inherited social and economic class. Some of us manage to cast off the religion into which we were born. We can choose to repudiate or embrace our ethnic heritage. We can celebrate or suppress our nationality. And even race—that great sore of American history—has become more fluid.[2]

Schwartz wrote this in 2004, but if he had written it today, I imagine he would add gender and sexual orientation to his list. He concludes that section by stating, "This change in the status of personal identity is both good and bad news: good news because it liberates us, and bad news because it burdens us with the responsibility of choice."[3]

Schwartz is absolutely right that this freedom is a blessing and a curse. On the one hand, many of the identities we receive are unhealthy and even oppressive. For centuries—millennia, really—women were thought to be less intelligent. Americans justified slavery by insisting on the objective inferiority of the African people they enslaved. To rid ourselves of these identities is not just freeing, but morally right.

On the other hand, the limitlessness of identity can become its own bondage. In the same way that we are overwhelmed by choice in other areas of our lives, the burden of creating our own identities can produce anxiety and stress as well.

The Therapeutic Self

New York pastor Tim Keller, who is a master at translating Scripture for our present culture, has recently turned his attention to this shift. In an interview in 2020, he explained that "the culture used to be about having the freedom to be your true self. More recently, it's about *creating* your own self."[4]

Drawing on the work of philosopher Charles Taylor, who coined the term "Therapeutic Self," Keller explained that according to the Therapeutic Self, we "are to look within at our desires—especially our sexual ones—and then determine who we are, not allowing anyone else to validate or define us or make us feel guilty."[5] In essence, the Therapeutic Self defines identity as "whatever makes you happy."

Keller calls this approach a "burden" for two reasons. The first is that our inner feelings or desires are not stable. Instead, they change throughout our lives. When you look back on your life and consider what you were like ten years ago, you were probably very different, and your goals have probably evolved. When I was a child, I wanted to be an archaeologist. When I started college, I wanted to major in psychology. For a long time as an adult, I thought I would focus on women's ministry. Today, I lead a church with my husband. My personality has changed as well. I used to be much more legalistic and less compassionate. These many, many changes raise the question, *Which one was my "true self"?* In each iteration of my dreams and personality, which one was the authentic *me*?

For all its talk of the true self, our culture has no reliable way to answer this question, or to assess when we have found it, other than a feeling. The standard is subjective, which means the target many people are pursuing is a moving one. For Christians, however, the standard is stable and clear. Our true self comes from Christ, and he is the standard by which we gauge our authenticity.

However, this does not mean we will all look the same. C. S. Lewis famously put it this way,

> The more we get what we now call "ourselves" out of the way and let Him take us over, the more truly ourselves we become. There is

so much of Him that millions and millions of "little Christs," all different, will still be too few to express Him fully. He made them all. He invented—as an author invents characters in a novel—all the different men that you and I were intended to be. In that sense our real selves are all waiting for us in Him.[6]

This measure of authenticity provides us with boundaries, but not the kind that produce a cookie-cutter faith. As Lewis explained so brilliantly, God is infinite, which means there is an infinite number of ways we reflect him. The more we become like Christ and prune away our sin, the more we align with the particular picture of Christ that God intended us to bear. In contrast, the Therapeutic Self has no boundaries to guide us. It is identity anarchy, and that is the first reason Keller calls it a burden.

The second reason is that the Therapeutic Self is "performative." This aspect of the modern self is probably best captured by the popular phrase "Pics or it didn't happen." If your true self isn't expressed, seen, or *public*, then you are not fully yourself. If your true self is not observable to others, then you are not fully you. Authenticity, then, is not just about figuring out who you are, but acting it out. And this, Keller rightly concludes, is exhausting.

The quest to find one's true self, with no other guidance but a feeling, and then live that self out fully is another mirage in the desert of self-help. It's difficult to know if and when you have ever arrived, especially when influences like depression or overwhelm affect the way you feel.

What makes this pursuit of "authenticity" even more challenging is social media. When young people scroll through their feeds, it would appear that almost everyone else has "found themselves," are expressing themselves fully, and are reaping all the rewards of that journey. In reality, social media is deceptive, and what we are seeing is not always real. As often as folks celebrate their life choices, they are less prone to share their mistakes, their regrets, or their ongoing struggles with self-doubt and self-loathing. Our culture lacks the language to admit, "I followed my dream and pursued my true self, and it went horribly." We refuse to label the quest for the true self as anything other than noble and good, no matter how one goes about it or how terribly it goes awry.

I realize this can all sound like a finger-wagging reprimand of our culture, and I want you to know I don't mean it to be. The reason our language about identity really concerns me is that it can obscure what is really going on in people's hearts. Behind the happy pictures and captions about being their true selves are, very often, people still in pain. The search for their true selves has not yielded the confidence they hoped it would, so in this final chapter on the various costs of control, let's look at the primary cost of controlling our identities.

The Cost: Elusive Peace

Like many of the topics in this book, the ability to experience freedom in our identities is actually very good. Having freedom in our identities is a long overdue correction to the narrow, culturally conditioned identities of the past. This correction is also biblical. In 1 Corinthians 12, Paul uses a metaphor of a body to capture the vast diversity of the church, a vision that the church has not always taken seriously:

> For just as the body is one and has many parts, and all the parts of that body, though many, are one body—so also is Christ. . . . Indeed, the body is not one part but many. If the foot should say, "Because I'm not a hand, I don't belong to the body," it is not for that reason any less a part of the body. And if the ear should say, "Because I'm not an eye, I don't belong to the body," it is not for that reason any less a part of the body. If the whole body were an eye, where would the hearing be? If the whole body were an ear, where would the sense of smell be? But as it is, God has arranged each one of the parts in the body just as he wanted. (vv. 12, 14–18)

Paul is saying something quite radical here, with serious implications for how we discern who God created us to be. Like the human body, the body of Christ has eyes, ears, legs, arms, hands, and feet—none of which resemble one another and all of which depend on one another to be healthy. The ear cannot function as an elbow, and the elbow cannot function as an ear, which is why we need to discern which "part" God created us to be. Until we understand this, we may mistakenly imitate someone else's role, instead of our own. We will also fail to serve the church as fully as God intended. This is why knowing your "part" matters so much. The particularity of *you* has a valuable role to play in the larger body of Christ.

Historically, our notions of identity have departed from this vision in two restricting ways: The first is by putting on someone else's identity instead of discovering our own. The second temptation is the reverse: wanting everyone to be the same as us. Some elbows want everyone to be elbows. Some arms want everyone to be arms. Some knees want everyone to be knees. Christians who are passionate about justice are sometimes wary of Christians passionate about evangelism, and vice versa. Rather than view one another as different parts of the same body, we act as if our little piece of the church represents the whole.

When we have this mentality, we end up dismissing or belittling other Christians with different callings and gifts. It is like the shoulder declaring, "Because the toes are not like me, they are not part of the body at all." This bad theology has unnecessarily limited our notions of identity, especially when combined with cultural expectations based on gender, race, and class.

At the same time, identity anarchy is not the answer either. When literally any identity is available to us, we saddle ourselves with overwhelming choice and all the anxiety it entails. In addition to that, we sentence ourselves to the hamster wheel of "maybe then," which goes like this:

I thought this job would bring me joy, but it hasn't, so I am going to try another. *Maybe then* I will feel satisfied.

I thought this dream would satisfy me, but it doesn't, so I need to chase after another. *Maybe then* I will feel content.

I thought this relationship would resolve my insecurities, but it hasn't, so I am going to try another. *Maybe then* I will stop feeling like I am not good enough.

The empty hope of "maybe then" has led many to pursue more money or more career advancement in order to feel satisfied. But our generation has added another type of "maybe then" to the list. This time, it is about identity:

I thought this version of myself would feel right, but I feel just as empty and unsure of myself as ever, so I need to find another. *Maybe then* I will feel at home in myself.

The open-endedness of this hope highlights the core difference between pursuing our God-given identity and the vague, direction-less journey of "following our dreams." One is tethered to something secure, and the other is not. One has a specific destination and the other has only a hypothetical one. That is not to say our particularities don't matter—1 Corinthians 12 affirms that they do!—but these particularities, which are so subject to change, cannot serve as the foundations of our identities. We need something more stable in order to feel secure.

A Better Way to Find Ourselves

Over the years I have written a lot about calling and how to discern it. I have also written a lot about 1 Corinthians 12, because it is such an essential vision for the church. Discerning our gifts and our identities is wise work.

And yet, even this emphasis on calling has pitfalls. When we overemphasize the importance of discovering our talents, even while using biblical language, we set ourselves up for shame and disappointment when our life circumstances prevent us from using our gifts. Maybe your gift is administration (and you LOVE it), but you have a child with special needs who requires your full attention at home. Maybe your gift is teaching Scripture, but you are already working two jobs to make ends meet and you can't add another commitment. Maybe your gift is service, but you suffer from chronic, debilitating pain that prevents you from doing much of anything. As all-encompassing as these situations are, none of them alter or undermine your God-given identity. And this matters greatly, because we *must* have an understanding of identity and the "true self" that is not diminished by factors like finances, schedules, or season of life. Otherwise, all that we are really talking about is the American dream of self-fulfillment, not the Christian vision of life in Christ. What we need is both an authentic sense of our God-given selves *and* an identity that does not change with the given day.

Both of those things can be found only in Christ, which is why Keller describes the Christian identity as one that is "received, not achieved."[7] No matter our circumstances, no matter our health, no matter our finances, no matter our culture, no matter our gender, and no matter our stage in life, our identity in Christ remains the same. There will never be a time when we are not chosen, approved, loved, and hoped for. We will always be his, so our task is not to reinvent the wheel of our identities, but to grow into our truest selves by becoming more and more like Jesus.

A Prayer of Repentance

Creator God, you know who you designed me to be. Before I took my first breath, you knew every day of my life. You knew your entire will for me. I am grateful for the gifts you wove into my being, but I also confess that sometimes I look to them for purpose before I look to you. I repent of placing any role, any worldly identity, no matter how good, above my identity as a child of God. I repent of serving those identities before I served you. And I affirm that the only identity that will truly set me free is the identity I received from your Son, Jesus Christ. He is my truest self.
Amen.

Questions for Self-Examination

1. Besides your faith, what are the top three things you find your identity in? Hint: Think about how you might write your bio on social media or introduce yourself to someone new.

2. Has the process of discerning who you are and what you are called to in life been easy or hard? Why?

3. Is there any part of your identity that you have tried to control by making yourself into who you *wanted* to be or what was *expected* of you?

4. In what ways have you seen the Holy Spirit transform you to look more like Christ?

PART IV

The REAL
Power God
Promises

14

The Power of Agency

I've devoted nearly an entire book to naming the problem of control, and now it's time to answer the big remaining question: What do we do when we feel out of control? Once we discern the temptation to control, in all its forms, what is our alternative?

For too long, my answer to this question was biblical but also unhelpful. I would simply resolve to "trust God more." I would remind myself that God is in control and I am not, so I need to surrender control to him.

Every bit of that solution is true and theologically accurate, but I also have to be honest and admit it hasn't done me much good. *Knowing* something is true is not the same as living it, which is why the mere knowledge of God's power has not changed my behavior terribly much. For all of us, trusting God instead of ourselves means resisting the inward-drifting gravity of our sinful natures *and* resisting the structure of our lives. Even if we want to release control, our smartphones constantly undermine us, promising information and predictability all day long. How, then, do we resist the "discipleship" of our culture, which reassures us, nearly every waking hour, of our own control?

Scripture has an answer to this problem, one with the practical handles we need for trusting God when we feel out of control. Once I discovered this answer, it provided me with direction and a sense of personal power, and I have returned to its truth again and again:

God does not give us control, but he does give us agency.

This distinction is essential to understand, because—as we have spent this entire book establishing—God does not give us control over much of anything. We cannot control the weather. We cannot control our health. We cannot control who our children grow up to be. We cannot control what other people think about us. We cannot control if our friends stay married. We cannot control if an economic downturn ruins our small business. We cannot even control ourselves! Not entirely, anyway. In Romans 7:15, Paul groans against his struggle with sin, confessing, "What I want to do I do not do, but what I hate I do" (NIV). There is so much that we cannot control, but in nearly all things, we *can* exercise agency.

Agency, which I will define as "the power to influence ourselves and our circumstances," is less absolute than control. It operates within limits. This concept acknowledges our role as partners with God, while submitting to the order of creation. Agency is what Adam and Eve enjoyed in the garden before the fall. While they did not possess unlimited freedom, knowledge, or power, they did have free will and influence. They partnered with God in bringing order out of chaos and exercising dominion over the world. They were neither all-powerful nor powerless.

The difference between control and agency is the difference between accepting our limitations and constantly thrashing against them. When we relinquish control in favor of agency, we set down the influence God has not given us to pick up the influence he has.

Agency—in the way I am using it here—is a psychological concept that does not appear explicitly in Scripture, but I chose it for a couple of reasons. The first is that it comes close to capturing the mysterious partnership we have with the Holy Spirit. The intersection of the Spirit's power and human ability is complex, but I think the concept of agency is a helpful category for understanding it.

The second reason I like this term is that it encompasses biblical concepts like freedom and self-control, but with clarifying boundaries. It acknowledges the full scope of our influence while submitting to the God-given limits of that influence. As an example of this, I prefer to speak of "agency over our bodies" as opposed to "control." We do not actually have control over our bodies—not in the sense that we can prevent them from aging or getting sick—but we do have agency. We can exercise. We can eat well. But we cannot control whether or not we get cancer.

Drawing on the previous section of the book, here are a few more examples of how this difference between control and agency plays out in various areas of our lives.

	CONTROL	AGENCY
RELATIONSHIPS	Manipulate; pressure; coerce; strong-arm; force	Provide wise counsel; support and encourage; pray
CIRCUMSTANCES	Overwork; obsessively plan; cut ethical corners; cheat	Plan, prepare, and execute conscientiously; act within the boundaries of sabbath; maintain a biblical moral code and a well-ordered life
REPUTATION	Cultivate a false image; manage what other people think about you	Culitvate integrity; be the same person in public that you are in private

Once I understood the difference between control and agency, I was able to reframe situations in which I felt out of control. Rather than frantically trying to seek control through more information, or through force, I instead asked, "What does it mean to exercise my Holy Spirit–powered agency?"

In 2 Timothy 1:7, Paul writes, "For God has not given us a spirit of fear, but one of power, love, and sound judgment." This is agency in a nutshell. God has not given us control, but he has given us other forms of influence. The more we exercise the power God has given us, instead of fruitlessly grasping for the power he has not, the more steadied and capable we will feel.

So, what does this look like practically? We don't have to look any further than the opening chapters of Genesis for the answer. Chapters 2 and 3 provide a blueprint of the agency God bestowed upon humanity, which they exercised in perfect freedom for the good of creation and themselves. What follows are the six forms of agency that we see in those chapters.

Naming and Ordering

Whenever I am anxious, I clean.

It is how I cope with chaos. When my life is running at a frantic pace or my children won't stop fighting or I am stressed about something at church, I redirect my emotions into organizing our home. I clear off the counters. I re-seal the granite. I scrub away all the scuff marks on our hallway walls and doors. I dig the trash out from under my kids' beds. I give away the clothes that don't fit them any longer. And when I am really stressed, I sort all of my kids' LEGOs by color.

There is something about a clean house that is deeply satisfying! I can think more clearly and breathe more deeply when everything is in its place, but like I said, this is also a coping mechanism. Rather than confront my control issues, I clean, and for years I felt guilty about this. I even wondered if my desire to clean our house was actually a *bad* thing.

Now I see it a bit differently.

While there are certainly days when I clean my house as a diversion, or in order to gain some sense of control over my life, what I now understand is that I do this because it is exactly what God created me to do. One of God's very first acts of creation was to order the universe. Genesis 1:2 tells us that the earth was formless and dark, and out of this nothing God created something in an orderly fashion. Rather than creating the world like an artist flinging paint across a canvas, God created systematically. He named his creation, he ordered it into a seven-day rhythm, and then he invited Adam to do the same. Adam's first job, in fact, was to assist God in this work of ordering, by naming the animals in the garden.

As creatures made in the image of God, this urge to name and order reflects God's character and his ways. It is how we exercise dominion in the world, and it sheds a beautiful light on seemingly utilitarian systems like a city's infrastructure. Roads and sewage pipes don't seem like God-glorifying inventions, but there is a very real sense in which they are.

So, how do we practice this form of agency? In two ways.

Naming

When God commissioned Adam to name the animals in the garden, it served a practical purpose. Adam could keep referring to "that giant gray animal with the long nose and tusks" or he could shorten it to "elephant." This naming saved time and made communication easier, but it also pointed to the higher purpose of naming, which is to identify exactly what we are talking about.

As I mentioned in the introduction, one primary function of this book is to name, because naming is powerful. Whether it is determining the right medical diagnosis, identifying a pattern in your life, or finally acknowledging an experience as abuse, the simple act of naming something *correctly* has the power to disarm and demystify. Until we take this important step, we will be tossed around by anonymous influences that we do not understand. Naming tames these forces.

Ordering

In our house, each one of our kids has his or her own shoe basket. All three baskets are located in the mudroom by the side entrance to our house, and whenever the kids come home, they put their shoes in their corresponding basket (well, in theory anyway). This system is meant to curb the time-squandering process of finding their shoes in whatever haphazard place they left them last, which we used to do every time we left the house. Now, we know exactly where they are.

Barry Schwartz calls organizational structures like this "second order decisions," which he defines as making "decisions about when to make decisions."[1] Rather than look for the shoes every time you leave, rather than go to the grocery store without a list, rather than wake up every morning with no plan whatsoever, you can limit the flood of choices you face each day by organizing your life through systems, processes, habits, and rhythms.

When we organize our lives using these second order decisions, we "limit the decisions we face and we can make life more manageable,"[2] which relieves us of a surprising amount of emotional and mental drain. That is one reason why the Christian faith itself is structured around a calendar and liturgies. Rhythms of faith like weekly corporate worship, bedtime prayers with our children, Advent, Lent—these all promote our spiritual growth without requiring any planning or decision-making.

In a world of overwhelming choice, ordering our lives is a powerful form of agency. Whether you are designing new processes for your small business, making a six-month plan for your family, or designing a family laundry system, you are imitating your creator. Like any good thing, order can become an idol of control, but it is also God's literal answer to chaos.

When life is too much and you feel out of control, stop and reflect on what's really going on inside you (name it!), and then consider what systems or structures might solve the problem (order it!).

Creating

After Adam finished naming the animals, Genesis 2:20 tells us that "no helper was found corresponding to him," so God created one. However, quite notably, God did not create this new person like he did before. Rather than breathe life into the dust, God *involved* Adam in the work of creating, by forming Eve directly from Adam's rib.

When I first began studying this chapter of the Bible, I missed this form of human agency for the simple reason that Adam was asleep the whole time. At first glance, he doesn't seem to be exercising any agency at all! But the truth is God was perfectly capable of creating Eve without Adam's help, which means it is no coincidence that God involved him. From the very beginning, God asserted that humans were "made in his image." And what is this God, in whose image we are made, like? Well, in Genesis 1 and 2 we see that his primary activity is creating. To be "made in his image," then, is to be made to create, and God confirmed this design when he included Adam in the creation of Eve.

Creating is a powerful form of agency, because it means we can literally change the world we live in. We may not be able to fix all the problems around us, but we can imagine and build creative solutions with true and long-lasting impact. At the same time, creating is not purely functional; it is also meaningful. When life is stressful or uncertain or chaotic, we can funnel our feelings into painting a canvas or building a piece of furniture or cooking a delicious meal. These "creative" options may seem unrelated or impractical, but they can actually have a healing effect, because "creating" is what God purposed us to do. Whenever we feel overwhelmed by the unpredictability of our lives, this form of agency invites us to put down control and pick up imagination, possibility, and beauty instead.

Setting Limits

This form of agency overlaps with ordering, because structure, by its very nature, is *limiting*. Not surprisingly, we see this in the garden. Adam and Eve were not granted endless choices. God did not permit them to eat of all the trees, but instead gave them a boundary. Likewise, God did not assign Adam to every task in the garden, but instead gave him very specific instructions to name the animals. Adam and Eve were free because of their limits, not in spite of them, and this is another needed expression of our agency: restoring our limits so we can thrive.

The previous section covered some of this already, because daily, weekly, and yearly rhythms constrain our lives in life-giving ways. The absence of these rhythms is another reason why the pandemic was so emotionally draining: we lost our structure. Prior to the pandemic, most of our plans and daily habits had already been set, which meant we didn't have to give much thought to them. But the pandemic forced us to reset *everything*, and the longer we lived in flux, with new guidelines about gatherings and travel and social distancing, the less bandwidth we had overall. It was all being spent on decision-making, which is why we need the stabilizing limitation of structure in our lives.

But these aren't the only limitations we need. In chapter 3 of this book, we saw how the deluge of information drowns us whenever we open our phones, and we need to limit this. We need less time on social media and less time reading the news.

Another important way to practice limiting is by limiting our yeses. Many of us are overwhelmed because we say yes to too much—our kid's school fundraiser, the meeting at night when we are supposed to be with our family, another commitment at church. Author Andy Crouch exemplified this limiting well, writing, "I have to say 'no' to requests many, many times a day. Almost always people are understanding. They often say, 'I know you are very busy.' The truth is I am NOT very busy. I try not to be busy at all. But in order for that to be true, I have to say 'no' many, many times a day."[3]

And finally, we can use our agency simply to embrace our limits. As we age, as our health declines, as we run out of energy, and as we hit our capacity, we can reject these boundaries by trying to control our bodies or our circumstances. Or we can receive these limits as gifts. Any time we are invited to unburden ourselves of the illusion of control and to remember that God is God and we are not, it is an opportunity for lighter living.

Practicing Care

In Genesis 2:15 (NIV), God commissions Adam to work the garden but also to "care" for it. It is easy to dismiss the importance of this because there is so much in nature we cannot control (hurricanes, earthquakes, volcanic eruptions, plagues), but this commission nevertheless assigns us a level of responsibility. A raging forest fire might begin with a discarded cigarette or a bolt of lightning, but it is wise and effective stewardship to reduce the number of fires when we can. This framework of creation care has endless applications.

That said, caring for creation is about more than the environment. Creation also includes our bodies. As a part of God's creation, our bodies are included in the command to "care," and this is another alternative to control. As I mentioned earlier, we cannot control our body type or the illnesses we contract, but we can care for our bodies. When we do, it is an act of stewardship over the one part of creation that most closely reflects God.

Praying

In the garden, Adam and Eve enjoyed uninterrupted, uninhibited communion with God. They could talk to God whenever they wanted, no matter the time of day, and we have the same access to God today, through prayer. Prayer is another form of human agency that has existed since the very beginning, but it is an agency that Adam and Eve ultimately failed to use. When the serpent misrepresented God and coaxed them to disobey, they should have run to God immediately. They should have brought their confusion and concerns to their Father, but because they chose their own way, they brought disaster onto themselves and to the world.

Whenever control entices us with its promises of knowledge and predictability, we face the same choice. Will we use our agency to go to God in prayer, or will we engineer an outcome of our own choosing?

I will be the first to admit how frequently I choose the latter. When I am worried about my kids or anxious about something at church or frustrated with a person in my life, I will spend entire days turning it over in my head, trying to figure out the solution. Then, at some point in the middle of my ruminating, it will dawn on me: "Oh! I can PRAY about this!"

Throughout this book I have argued that the problem with control is not simply that it doesn't work, but that it makes things even worse. It makes difficult situations more complicated. It makes strained relationships more precarious. But when we find ourselves headed down that path toward destruction, prayer is what pulls us back. Whenever we feel the urge to control a situation, we can take it to God in prayer before we do even more damage on our own.

I wonder how many needless consequences of control could have been avoided if we had only taken our cares to God first. I wonder how many ugly words or hurtful conversations could have been avoided had we started by seeking God in prayer.

Sometimes the effect of prayer is not to change someone else or to ensure a specific outcome, but to stop ourselves from sinning. It is a sorely neglected form of agency, which is why I included it in every chapter of this book. The most basic starting point for resisting our craving for control is prayer.

Self-Examining

The final form of agency that we can and must practice if we are to confront the idolatry of control in our lives is self-examination. This is also the second form of agency that is neglected in Genesis 3. The first, as we just saw, was going directly to God. In verses 9 and 13, God invites Adam and Eve to practice this second form of agency when he asks them the following two questions: *Where are you?* and *What have you done?*

Both questions are rhetorical, because God already knew where they were, and he knew exactly what they had done. Instead, these questions were for *their benefit.* In this moment, God was asking Adam and Eve to be truthful with themselves about what they had done and why, and both were unable to do so.

Self-examination seems completely unrelated to control, but it is the first step necessary to even recognize our idolatry of control and take the steps to change. My hope is that this entire book has been a companion in that work. Like a doctor taking an X-ray, we cannot know what is broken without looking inside ourselves, which is why God poses the same questions to us today: *Where are you?* and *What have you done?* Are you afraid? Uncertain? Angry? Confused? How have you acted out of your feelings? And how might you live from a posture of trust today?

A Greater Power Than Agency

Although the word *agency* is not explicitly biblical, I believe it is a direct extension of having a soul. That is to say, you cannot have agency without a soul, which is why we do not speak of animals as having agency. Sure, some animals have the ability to organize and even plan, but these behaviors are driven by *instinct* rather than *agency.* Animals cannot self-examine. Animals cannot pray. Animals do not possess truly free will.

In that sense agency is one of the things that distinguishes us as unique creations who bear the image of God. We were neither de-signed to be robots, nor animals driven by instinct. We can dream, we can laugh, we can confess our struggles, and we can empathize. We have a freedom and independence that no other creature has.

That is just my opinion on how agency fits into Scripture and a theology of humankind, but what is *not* my opinion is this: after the fall, every shred of creation was broken and nothing was left untouched. Everything that God had created needed to be redeemed, and that includes the human will. Although God gave us the freedom to be in relationship with him and to participate in tending creation, we struggle to do this. Our wills—including our agency—are broken.

Thankfully, when we become one in Christ, God begins the work of repairing all that was undone. He heals our shame and restores our relationship with him. He also liberates our wills from the bondage of sin and corrects our agency through the power of the Holy Spirit. Every form of agency—naming, ordering, creating, limiting, caring, praying, and self-examining—is made possible by his power, not our own, and that is a relief, because rejecting the idol of control is HARD. There are so many days when nothing in me wants to do this. I want to force my own outcome. I don't want to wait. I don't want the uncertainty. I don't want the pain. And control is sitting right there in front of me like the perfect solution.

Left to our own devices, we would repeat the sin of the fall forever, like a record on repeat. But praise God he hasn't left us to our own devices. Instead, he sent his Spirit to help us, and it is this— not our self-discipline or our hard work or even our faithfulness— that rescues us from the trap of control. For any soul reading this who is tired of the bondage of control and simply wants to be free of it, hear the good news: that desire, in and of itself, means the Spirit of the living God is already at work inside you.

A Prayer of Petition

Holy Spirit, I do not always want what you want. I like my control. I like being in the driver's seat of my life. I think I know what is best and I hate to wait. This is why I am asking you to change my heart. Sober me with the knowledge of my own limitations. Convict me of the consequences of control.

Turn my heart to your will and your ways and away from the folly of trusting my own. Empower me to exercise my God-given agency instead of seeking after control. Thank you that I do not have to do any of this in my own might, because I can take up the easy yoke of Jesus instead.
    Amen.

Questions for Self-Examination

1. What form of control do you need to name?

2. What is the number one thing that you need to limit in your life right now so that you can better "order" your time, attention, and schedule?

3. Where are you today? God asked Adam and Eve this question in Genesis 3, and it is a powerful prayer of self-examination to start each day. Take some time to reflect on where you are today, especially in relation to control.

15

The One Thing
We Can Control

One morning Ike and I sat across from each other at our kitchen table, unpacking our feelings about a painful situation at church. We were both equally frustrated about it, but we handle our frustrations differently. Ike is an internal processor, so he withdraws inside himself, thinks, and occasionally broods. I do not do that. I am a verbal processor, and I am loud. I articulate every single reason why I think someone hurt us or why a plan failed. I fume and fume until I have run out of things to say, and then, after the heat has finally burned off, I turn to Ike and ask, "How can I help you with this? What do you need?"

That morning, Ike responded to this question in a way he never had before. He said, "Honestly, this situation is hard, but what makes it the hardest for me is *you*. Your response makes me feel like I need to do something to make it better right now, because I don't want you to be this upset."

Stunned, I blinked a couple times. "Oh!"

Ike continued, "If you really want to help me, I need you to figure out how to process your anger without exploding on me."

Of course, Ike was exactly right. I was taking out my control issues on him instead of taking them to God. Rather than venting my anger to the Lord before venting to anyone else, Ike was getting the full brunt of my raw, unfiltered emotions, and it made it difficult for him to process his own. While there is a lot about our church that I cannot control, I was doing very little to control the one thing I could.

The Role of Self-Control

This entire book has been about how very little control we have in our lives and the fallout of refusing to accept this. If there is one message I want you to take from this book, it's that control is a devil's deal. It does not work the way you think it will. It cannot give you the outcome you want it to. Every time you are faced with the temptation to control, I want this refrain ringing in your ears:

When I use control to fix things, it only breaks them more.

Whether it is our broken circumstances or our own anxiety, control does not resolve the problem, but only makes it worse. I believe this to my bones, because I have experienced it personally and Scripture affirms it. We were not created to control.

But this leaves us with one final question. Does this mean we control *nothing*? According to Scripture, yes and no.

The word *self-control* appears periodically throughout the Bible. In the Old Testament it appears twice, exclusively in the book of Proverbs:

> Better a patient person than a warrior,
>   one with self-control than one who takes a city. (16:32 NIV)

> Like a city whose walls are broken through
>   is a person who lacks self-control. (25:28 NIV)

In both of these examples, *self-control* is not the exact translation of the Hebrew but is instead shorthand for "restraining one's spirit." In the New Testament, *self-control* appears much more often, most commonly as the Greek word *sōphrōn*, which means "curbing one's desires and impulses, self-controlled, temperate." Or it is the word *enkrateia*, which literally means "in strength" or "in power" but is best translated as "self-control." Below is a sample of the contexts where these two Greek terms appear:

> But the fruit of the Spirit is love, joy, peace, forbearance, kindness, goodness, faithfulness, gentleness and self-control. Against such things there is no law. (Gal. 5:22–23 NIV)

> People will be lovers of themselves, lovers of money, boastful, proud, abusive, disobedient to their parents, ungrateful, unholy, without love, unforgiving, slanderous, without self-control, brutal, not lovers of the good, treacherous, rash, conceited, lovers of pleasure rather than lovers of God. (2 Tim. 3:2–4 NIV)

> Rather, [an overseer] must be hospitable, one who loves what is good, who is self-controlled, upright, holy and disciplined. (Titus 1:8 NIV)

> For this very reason, make every effort to add to your faith goodness; and to goodness, knowledge; and to knowledge, self-control; and to self-control, perseverance; and to perseverance, godliness; and to godliness, mutual affection; and to mutual affection, love. (2 Pet. 1:5–7 NIV)

Based on these passages, Tim Keller defines self-control as the ability to "choose the important thing rather than the urgent thing."[1] I might feel an urgent need to get a new outfit for a special occasion. Alcoholics might feel an urgent need for a drink. If you are dating someone, you might feel an urgent need to be physically close to them. But self-control asks, "What is more *important?*"

Getting the new outfit or saving money? Having the drink or maintaining sobriety? Having sex with someone you are not married to or honoring them, yourself, and God by abstaining?

Scripture tells us that we have the power to choose the important. Unlike animals, we are not controlled by instincts and urges, and what the passage in Galatians clarifies is that this power comes not from us, but from the Holy Spirit.

So yes, we do have control! Because of our God-given agency, we have the control to make choices about our character and who we want to be. Because we have self-control, we are not captive to our worst impulses.

But we do not have total control. Not yet. As I mentioned in an earlier chapter, Paul laments his lack of self-control in Romans 7:

> For I do not understand what I am doing, because I do not practice what I want to do, but I do what I hate. Now if I do what I do not want to do, I agree with the law that it is good. So now I am no longer the one doing it, but it is sin living in me. (vv. 15–17)

This passage indicates that our self-control is inhibited. Our self-control is not absolute, because we are still sinners. Every day the Holy Spirit makes us more and more like Christ, but that transformation, which is also called "sanctification," is not complete, and one sign of this incomplete spiritual growth is our incomplete self-control. Sometimes we know what we ought to do, and maybe we even want to do it, but we don't.

This means we must hold two realities in tension: The only thing we have control over is ourselves, and even that control is incomplete.

The latter truth can feel a bit like the fly in the ointment, but together, these two truths empower us without condemning us when we fail. On the one hand, the many verses about self-control assure us that we have agency and power in ourselves. We can say no to toxic habits or destructive relationships. We can say yes to a healthy lifestyle and a flourishing faith. Because of the Holy Spirit, we possess the capacity to take real, meaningful steps.

At the same time though, we are not perfect. Our sanctification has not been completed, and there is grace for this. God knows we are in process. He has instilled us with everything we need to practice self-control. The Holy Spirit can help us stop visiting inappropriate websites, bite our tongue instead of gossiping with our coworkers, and walk out of the room instead of exploding on our kids, but God also knows how difficult it is to practice this self-control in view of sin. It is both/and. We have power and we have grace, and neither is ultimately rooted in us. From start to finish the exercise of self-control is fueled by the Holy Spirit.

With all of that in mind, I want to look at a few ways we can choose self-control when we feel tempted to control others, our circumstances, our bodies, our reputations, and our identities. In the heat of the moment, when we feel helpless or anxious or desperate to fix things, God does not simply ask us to release control, but to practice self-control, which means choosing between the following options.

Placing Blame or Taking Responsibility

One of the weird ways we cope with our lack of control is through blame. I say weird, because blame is another counterintuitive form of control, though it has been with us since the garden, and I can even give you an example of it from my life this week. Over the weekend we invited some friends to the local pool. We checked the weather and the hourly report said there was a 0 percent chance of rain, so we loaded up our gear and headed down the street. About thirty minutes after we got there, we noticed dark clouds looming on the horizon. Soon we heard a clap of thunder and the pool shut down for half an hour. Not long after that, it began to rain.

I rechecked my phone and, sure enough, the weather forecast had changed to a 70 percent chance of rain. I stared at this new information and began to growl at my phone: "This weather app is worthless! What good is a forecast if it is going to change within minutes of the storm?" I was responding to my weather app as if it was meant to possess the foresight of God himself and should render predictions accordingly. What I was *really* doing was reckoning with my lack of control. I had expected my tiny weather app to give me something it could not—infallibility—and I blamed it when it failed.

This is a common response when we experience things beyond our control. When the power goes out or we get a flat tire or the Starbucks line takes too long, we cope with it by blaming something. Anything. I have constructed entire personality profiles about strangers who were driving too slowly in front of me. This compulsion is so strong because it's easy. It's easier to throw an internal tantrum than submit these experiences to God as opportunities for growth.

Blame does not immediately present itself as a control issue, but as we already saw in our discussion of the prosperity gospel, it's a common one. If we can blame someone for their misfortune, it means we can prevent it from happening to us. Similarly, if we can pinpoint who's to blame for the problems in our country, then the whole world feels a lot less unpredictable and capricious. Blaming means we have a handle on it. In fact, this was a common narrative in the pandemic: it must be *somebody's* fault. Because the alternative is much scarier to accept.

The problem is, blaming is mostly a distraction. Of course, there is a time for holding the right people accountable, but when your flight is delayed or your internet goes down or the grocery store runs out of your favorite brand of ice cream, blame is just a distraction from the reality of your lack of control.

There is a popular saying that I have heard many times, and you probably have too: **you cannot control what happens to you,**

but you can control how you respond. This is absolutely true. We have this power because of human agency and the spiritual fruit of self-control. We do not have to lash out when our illusions of control begin to falter. Instead, we can take responsibility for our own responses by

- admitting our limitations,
- acknowledging our frustration,
- praying for God's help,
- remembering God's goodness, and
- affirming that we can trust him.

And then, if any additional action is warranted, we can respond under the bridle of the Holy Spirit.

Responding Reactively or Listening Patiently

Although we cannot control people, that does not mean we are helpless to influence them. However, our ability to influence depends on how we respond.

Author Edwin Friedman pinpoints "reactivity" as one of the key ways we forfeit our influence. He defines reactivity as "the vicious cycle of intense reactions of each member to events and to one another."[2] You have probably experienced an interaction just like this. Maybe you offered unsolicited feedback to someone and they responded defensively. They threw the criticism back in your face and then accused you of something just as bad or worse. In response, you became even more defensive, and before you knew it, you were locked in a battle of escalating voices.

When this happens, both parties are attempting to win by controlling the other's perspective. But instead of influencing each other, they are only becoming more entrenched, more adversarial, and most likely, less rational. Like all forms of control, reactivity accomplishes the opposite of its goal.

I know this "vicious cycle" well because I am a fighter and I fight to win. It is a long-term, deep-seated personality trait of mine. Whenever I am in a conversation with someone with whom I strongly disagree, I am going to debate them. And if the topic is especially important and close to my heart, I can get pretty heated. I don't just want people to understand why they are wrong, but why Scripture is ON MY SIDE. And this does not, as you might imagine, go over well in meetings.

Ike, on the other hand, is not a reactive leader. In difficult meetings he remains as cool as a cucumber. He listens patiently. He waits and takes his time until he can discern the issue under the issue. I am the fish that lunges for the glittery lure and immediately gets caught on a hook. Ike circles and observes until he can see what's happening from every angle, which is why he almost never takes the bait.

As Friedman describes, reactivity compounds anxiety, which then feeds reactivity even more. He describes the telltale signs of a group stuck in this cycle:

> Members of chronically anxious [systems] will be quick to interrupt one another, if not to jump in and complete one another's sentences, and they are constantly taking and making things "personal." Communication is marked more by diagnostic or labeling "you" positions rather than by self-defining "I" statements.[3]

When I read that description, it reminded me so much of our culture today. Log on to social media and there it is! We are a reactive culture that is becoming more and more vicious by the day. But how do we stop it? Friedman argues that the only way to break this cycle is for someone to be a non-anxious presence. Rather than react, they listen, they remain sincere, they maintain a healthy emotional distance, they are appropriately playful, and they intentionally avoid reactive interactions.

When we are able do this, it has a surprising amount of influence, because it lowers the temperature of a conversation instead of raising it more. A non-anxious presence has the power to de-escalate a situation, while an anxious presence tends to ratchet it up. In my own marriage, Ike accomplishes this masterfully. Whenever our voices are rising and our emotions are fraying and I am increasingly fighting to win, he disarms the whole conflict by pausing a beat and calmly saying, "What I hear you saying is . . ." From there, he makes a sincere effort to hear and understand what I am saying, rather than react to what he doesn't like.

Listening is not a fail-safe influence. It does not guarantee that the other person will reciprocate or change their mind. But it can avoid the relational fallout of control. It is also just more faithful to Jesus. As often as the religious leaders tried to entrap Jesus and provoke him with trick questions about Scripture, Jesus could have responded reactively. He could have outargued them, and he could have been condescending. Instead, he listened to what they were really saying and discerned what was really behind their questions. Jesus did this with everyone, in fact. He listened to what was going on, and he responded accordingly. Because of this, the sincere in faith left his presence feeling heard, while the hypocrites felt exposed. In both cases, the ability to exercise self-control rather than to react was one way Jesus influenced his followers, and it must also be ours.

Gripping Tighter or Trusting the Driver

My sons are currently in a big *Jurassic World* phase. They are too young to watch the movies but they are obsessed with dinosaurs, so Ike and I recently watched the movies to find out which parts to show them and which to fast-forward through. All of the *Jurassic Park* and *Jurassic World* movies revolve around similar themes, namely the peril of scientific hubris and the limits of human control, and this is spelled out rather explicitly toward the beginning of the first *Jurassic World*. In one scene, the new owner of the park, Simon Masrani, takes his operations manager, Claire Dearing, on a helicopter ride. Masrani is a novice pilot, and as the helicopter jolts off the ground, Dearing braces herself in panic. With her feet spread wide and her arms sprawled across the cabin, Masrani glances back at her, chuckles, and says, "You look tense, Claire!" She suggests he focus on navigating the helicopter instead of looking back at her, and he calmly philosophizes, "The key to a happy life is to accept that you are never actually in control."[4]

It was a surprisingly accurate spiritual truth for a dinosaur movie! Masrani was right. Dearing could not have gripped the helicopter hard enough to make it safer. No matter how she positioned her body, no matter how tightly she held on, none of it made any difference to how the helicopter flew. Either the helicopter was safe or it wasn't. The only thing that really mattered was the competence of the one who was flying it.

Many of us go through life this way. We are frantically bracing ourselves, unable to accept our lack of control, as if gripping our circumstances tighter gives us greater influence than the One who orchestrates the cosmos. That said, God's response to our tightly wound, control freak selves is not merely a command to surrender. Instead, he lovingly looks upon us with warmth and compassion and says, "That grip of yours is strong and good. You're just grabbing onto the wrong thing."

The Deal of a Lifetime

This entire book has been, in many ways, one long meditation on Genesis 3. So much consequence was bound up in that single moment in history, and so much has transpired as a result. Jesus's death and resurrection were a mirror reversal of those events, but there is another key moment from Jesus's life that carries significance as well.

In Luke 4, Jesus has just been baptized and is about to com-
mence his ministry on earth. But first, the Spirit leads him into
the wilderness, where he remains isolated and fasts for forty days.
During that time the devil tempts Jesus with three different offers
(vv. 1–2).

First, the devil tempts Jesus to use his power to disobey. It was
the Holy Spirit who led Jesus into the wilderness to fast, so when
the devil taunts Jesus to turn a stone into a piece of bread, he
isn't merely demanding a parlor trick. What he is really trying to
provoke in Jesus is disobedience, and in Jesus's weakened state,
the idea has to be appealing. But as hungry as Jesus is, he would
rather obey God than eat, so he responds with Scripture and says
no to the devil (vv. 3–4).

Next, the devil offers Jesus authority over a wider domain if he
will just bow down and worship him. Again, we are left to wonder
if Jesus found the offer enticing, not because he needed the power,
but because he could have done a lot of good with it. Jesus would
have been a wonderful ruler, the best there ever was! But he turns
down this offer too, choosing to worship God alone (vv. 5–8).

Finally, the devil tempts Jesus to prove he is the Son of God by
throwing himself from the top of a building so that his angels can
catch him. Once again, Jesus rejects the offer, choosing to trust
God rather than test him (vv. 9–12).

In the Bible, three is a number of completion, and this story
contains three different deals with the devil. Three times Jesus
could have sold his soul and three times he did not.

What we have in this story is an alternate ending to Genesis 3.
We are seeing how it could have gone. How it *should* have gone.
In this story, Jesus is the perfect image of self-control. He obeys,
he rejects the temptation of power, and he debunks the lies of the
devil. He is doing all that Adam and Eve could not.

He is also doing what *we* cannot.

That is the good news of Jesus Christ, but it gets even better.
Not only does Jesus rewrite the story, but he also pays the debt.

Throughout this book we have looked at many individual "costs of control," but they are all pointing back to the original. In that first deal with the devil, when Adam and Eve traded paradise for power, the entire world suffered the cost of their sin.

But this very cost—the cost of *their* control—is why Jesus came to earth, lived, died, and rose again. He came to pay the cost, and that is the final truth I want to leave you with. I want you to understand, deep in your bones, that control always comes with a price. There is no exception, no shortcut, no escape clause to this principle. It is a rule as reliable as the sun.

But I also want you to understand that it is not the only offer on the table.

Jesus came to break the cycle of control. He came so that our story would not end in death, but life. And he came to show us that we don't have to settle for the devil's offers of security, success, and power anymore. We can have the real thing in Jesus.

A Prayer of Thanksgiving

Jesus, thank you for paying the cost of Adam's and Eve's sin, and mine as well. Thank you for paying the cost of control. Because you did, I don't have to negotiate with the devil. I don't have to bargain with control. I can experience the true freedom, the real power, and the abiding security that come from trusting in you. Thank you for offering me life.

Amen.

191

Questions for Self-Examination

1. Why do you think self-control is the only form of control that God allows us?

2. In your own life, how have you seen self-control as a form of influence?

3. Read Luke 4:1–13. What supported Jesus's self-control?

Acknowledgments

This book was supposed to be turned in a year ago—right in the thick of the pandemic—but my publisher, Baker Books, understood. They wanted me to write a book that was thoughtful and careful and Spirit-led, and I cannot thank them enough for their patience. Rebekah Guzman, in particular, has been an author's dream. I am so grateful I get to work with her whole team (including Stephanie Smith and Robin Turici).

To my husband, Ike, who cleared out our schedules so that I could go away and write for a week. I am the luckiest girl. Thank you for continuing to be my greatest advocate and my very best friend. I literally could not do any of this without you.

To my parents, who have showed up again and again to watch the kids and make time for me to write. I could not have dreamed of better parents. You are God's extravagant grace in my life, and I love you so much.

To K. J. Ramsey, Lindsay Geist, and Matt Conner, for taking the time to offer professional feedback on the psychology undergirding this book. Your wisdom has enriched these pages!

To my agent on this book, Jana Burson, who has been with me since my first book and is a big part of the reason I get to do this incredible work—thank you!

To Cherryel Scurry, who graciously offered her mountain cabin so that I could focus on this book. Your home was such a haven for my soul and the exact environment I needed to write this message well. Thank you for your lavish generosity!

And to Isaac, Coen, and Sadie, who do not care a bit about my books, but who are my greatest joy, every single day of my life. I could write a thousand books and it still wouldn't compare to the pride I feel over you.

Notes

Introduction

1. Philip R. Muskin, "What Are Anxiety Disorders?," American Psychiatric Association, June 2021, https://www.psychiatry.org/patients-families/anxiety-disorders/what-are-anxiety-disorders.
2. Susanna Calling et al., "Longitudinal Trends in Self-Reported Anxiety. Effects of Age and Birth Cohort during 25 Years," BMC Psychiatry 17, no. 119 (April 2017), https://doi.org/10.1186/s12888-017-1277-3.
3. Mary E. Duffy, Jean M. Twenge, and Thomas E. Joiner, "Trends in Mood and Anxiety Symptoms and Suicide-Related Outcomes among U.S. Undergraduates, 2007–2018: Evidence from Two National Surveys," Journal of Adolescent Health 65, no. 5 (November 2019), https://www.sciencedirect.com/science/article/abs/pii/S1054139X1930254X.
4. Jean M. Twenge, iGen: Why Today's Super-Connected Kids Are Growing Up Less Rebellious, More Tolerant, Less Happy—and Completely Unprepared for Adulthood—and What That Means for the Rest of Us (New York: Atria, 2017), 148.
5. Twenge, iGen, 148.
6. Twenge, iGen, 150.

Chapter 1 The Illusion of Control

1. Robert D. McFadden, "Harold Camping, Dogged Forecaster of the End of the World, Dies at 92," New York Times, December 17, 2013, https://www.nytimes.com/2013/12/18/us/harold-camping-radio-entrepreneur-who-predicted-worlds-end-dies-at-92.html.
2. McFadden, "Harold Camping."
3. Rick Paulas, "What Happened to Doomsday Prophet Harold Camping after the World Didn't End?," Vice, November 7, 2014, https://www.vice.com/en/article/yvqkwb/life-after-doomsday-456.
4. "List of Dates Predicted for Apocalyptic Events," Wikipedia, accessed February 17, 2022, https://en.wikipedia.org/wiki/List_of_dates_predicted_for_apocalyptic_events.

5. Sarah Hinlicky Wilson, from her interview on the podcast *Queen of the Sciences*, "Whether One May Flee from a Deadly Plague," March 27, 2020.

6. *Oxford English Dictionary*, s.v. "control," accessed January 11, 2022, https://www.lexico.com/en/definition/control.

7. *APA Dictionary of Psychology*, s.v. "control," accessed January 11, 2022, https://dictionary.apa.org/control.

8. Jennifer Dukes Lee, *It's All Under Control: A Journey of Letting Go, Hanging On, and Finding a Peace You Almost Forgot Was Possible* (Carol Stream, IL: Tyndale, 2018), 33.

9. A. H. Maslow, "A Theory of Human Motivation," *Psychological Review* 50, no. 4 (1943): 370–96, https://doi.org/10.1037/h0054346.

10. I want to credit Mark Sayers for helping me to make this connection. On his *Rebuilders* podcast, Sayers has periodically mentioned Maslow's placement of "control" in his Hierarchy of Needs, and this was the impetus for my own exploration of it.

11. E. J. Langer, "The Illusion of Control," *Journal of Personality and Social Psychology* 32, no. 2 (1975): 311–28, https://doi.org/10.1037/0022-3514.32.2.311.

12. Matthew W. Gallagher, Kate H. Bentley, and David H. Barlow, "Perceived Control and Vulnerability to Anxiety Disorders: A Meta-Analytic Review," *Cognitive Theory Research* 38 (June 2014): 571–84, https://doi.org/10.1007/s10608-014-9624-x.

13. Twenge, *iGen*, 167.

14. Jean Twenge on *The Carey Nieuwhof Leadership Podcast*, "Jean Twenge on Rising Anxiety, Depression, Isolation and Smartphones in Gen Z, and What That Means for Them and for Leaders," August 11, 2021, https://careynieuwhof.libsyn.com/cnlp-435-jean-twenge-on-rising-anxiety-depression-isolation-and-smartphones-in-gen-z-and-what-that-means-for-them-and-for-leaders.

15. Walter Brueggemann, *Reality, Grief, Hope: Three Urgent Prophetic Tasks* (Grand Rapids: Eerdmans, 2014).

Chapter 2 How We Got Here

1. Barry Schwartz, *The Paradox of Choice: Why More Is Less* (New York: HarperCollins, 2004), 2.

2. Acts 24:25, Galatians 5:23, and 2 Peter 1:6.

3. Steve Cuss, *Managing Leadership Anxiety: Yours and Theirs* (Nashville: Thomas Nelson, 2019), 20.

4. J. K. Rowling, *Harry Potter and the Sorceror's Stone* (Broadway, NY: Scholastic Inc., 1998).

5. Mark Sayers, *A Non-Anxious Presence: How a Changing and Complex World Will Create a Remnant of Renewed Christian Leaders* (Chicago: Moody, 2022), 38.

Chapter 3 Knowledge and Information

1. Edwin H. Friedman, *A Failure of Nerve: Leadership in the Age of the Quick Fix*, rev. ed. (New York: Church Publishing, 2017), loc. 115–16, Kindle.

2. Stephan Lewandowsky et al., "Misinformation and Its Correction: Continued Influence and Successful Debiasing," *Psychological Science in the Pub-*

lic Interest 13, no. 3 (December 2012):106–31, https://doi.org/10.1177/1529 100612451018.
3. Gregory J. Trevors et al., "Identity and Epistemic Emotions During Knowledge Revision: A Potential Account for the Backfire Effect," *Discourse Processes* 53, no. 5–6 (June 2016): 339–70, https://doi.org/10.1080/0163853X.2015.1136507.

Chapter 4 Power

1. Diane Langberg, *Redeeming Power: Understanding Authority and Abuse in the Church* (Grand Rapids: Baker Books, 2020), 5.
2. Langberg, *Redeeming Power*, 6.
3. Langberg, *Redeeming Power*, 6.
4. Langberg, *Redeeming Power*, 8.
5. Langberg, *Redeeming Power*, 63.
6. Langberg, *Redeeming Power*, 66.
7. Langberg, *Redeeming Power*, 171.

Chapter 5 Money

1. Mathias Nylandsted Benediktson, "Investigating the U-Shaped Charitable Giving Profile Using Register-Based Data," *Centre of Health Economics Research* 1 (2018): 34–35, https://ideas.repec.org/p/hhs/sduhec/2018_001.html.
2. Alessandra Malito, "The Unexpected Link between Social Status and Generosity," MarketWatch, July 7, 2018, https://www.marketwatch.com/story/the unexpected-link-between-social-status-and-generosity-2018-07-03.
3. Langberg, *Redeeming Power*, 68.
4. Langberg, *Redeeming Power*, 69.
5. Stanley Hauerwas, *Matthew: Brazos Theological Commentary on the Bible* (Grand Rapids: Brazos Press, 2006), 174.

Chapter 6 Autonomy

1. Paul Taylor, Cary Funk, and April Clark, "Americans and Social Trust: Who, Where and Why," Pew Research Center, February 22, 2007, https://www.pewresearch.org/social-trends/2007/02/22/americans-and-social-trust-who-where-and-why/.
2. David Brooks, "America Is Having a Moral Convulsion," *Atlantic*, October 5, 2020, https://www.theatlantic.com/ideas/archive/2020/10/collapsing-levels-trust-are-devastating-america/616581/.
3. Aaron Earls, "Americans' Trust of Pastors Hovers Near All-Time Low," LifeWay Research, January 22, 2021, https://lifewayresearch.com/2021/01/22/americans-trust-of-pastors-hovers-near-all-time-low/.
4. Earls, "Americans' Trust of Pastors."
5. Kavin Rowe, *Christianity's Surprise: A Sure and Certain Hope* (Nashville: Abingdon Press, 2020), 85.
6. Rowe, *Christianity's Surprise*, 85.
7. Schwartz, *The Paradox of Choice*, 107–8.
8. Brooks, "America Is Having a Moral Convulsion."

Chapter 7 Theology

1. Kate Bowler, *Everything Happens for a Reason: And Other Lies I've Loved* (New York: Random House, 2018), 170.
2. Bowler, *Everything Happens for a Reason*, xiii.
3. Bowler, *Everything Happens for a Reason*, xiv.

Chapter 8 Shame

1. David J. Ayers, "Sex and the Single Evangelical," Institute for Family Studies, August 14, 2019, https://ifstudies.org/blog/sex-and-the-single-evangelical.
2. Lisa Cannon Green, "Survey: Women Go Silently from Church to Abortion Clinic," Focus on the Family, August 17, 2021, https://www.focusonthefamily.com/pro-life/survey-women-go-silently-from-church-to-abortion-clinic/.

Chapter 9 Broken Relationships

1. Katie Frost, "7 Things to Know About Princess Margaret and Peter Townsend's Love Affair," Town & Country, December 8, 2017, https://www.townandcountrymag.com/society/tradition/news/a8139/princess-margaret-peter-townsend-love-affair/.
2. Eliana Dockterman and Suyin Haynes, "The True Story behind *The Crown*'s Prince Charles, Princess Diana and Camilla Parker Bowles Love Triangle," *Time*, November 15, 2020, https://time.com/5910567/diana-charles-camilla-the-crown/.
3. Cuss, *Managing Leadership Anxiety*, 93.
4. Cuss, *Managing Leadership Anxiety*, 95.
5. Steve Cuss (@stevecusswords), "3. Clarify responsibility," Twitter, October 14, 2020, https://twitter.com/stevecusswords/status/1316381063317315584.
6. Based on Steve Cuss (@stevecusswords), "The 4 spaces," Twitter, January 18, 2021, https://twitter.com/stevecusswords/status/1351183901750919173.

Chapter 10 Burnout

1. Anne Helen Peterson, *Can't Even: How Millennials Became the Burnout Generation* (Boston: Mariner, 2021), xxii.
2. Anne Helen Peterson, "How Millennials Became the Burnout Generation," *Buzzfeed News*, January 5, 2019, https://www.buzzfeednews.com/article/annehelenpetersen/millennials-burnout-generation-debt-work.
3. Peterson, *Can't Even*, ix.

Chapter 11 Body Shame

1. Angelica Xidias, "31 of the Craziest Celebrity Beauty Treatments," *Vogue Australia*, February 10, 2021, https://www.vogue.com.au/beauty/trends/20-of-the-craziest-celebrity-beauty-treatments/image-gallery/4dbd73767fb6985a63d1998e080da8d4.
2. K. J. Ramsey, *This Too Shall Last: Finding Grace When Suffering Lingers* (Grand Rapids: Zondervan, 2020), 31.
3. Lamar Hardwick, *Disability and the Church: A Vision for Diversity and Inclusion* (Westmont, IL: InterVarsity Press, 2021), 71.

4. Jess Connolly, *Breaking Free of Body Shame: Dare to Reclaim What God Has Named Good* (Grand Rapids: Zondervan, 2021).

5. Katherine Wolf and Jay Wolf, *Suffer Strong: How to Survive Anything by Redefining Everything* (Grand Rapids: Zondervan, 2020), 23.

Chapter 12 Anxiety

1. Steve Cuss, "The 4 Spaces."

Chapter 13 Exhaustion

1. Lulu Garcia-Navarro, "'There's No Map': Glennon Doyle On Living An 'Untamed' Life," NPR, Weekend Edition Sunday, March 22, 2020, https://www.npr.org/2020/03/22/818495802/theres-no-map-glennon-doyle-on-living-an-untamed-life#:~:text=I%20have%20a%20boy%20and,to%20them%2C%20is%20anybody%20hungry%3F&text=There's%20decisions%20that%20we%20can,can%20call%20our%20friends%20about.

2. Schwartz, *The Paradox of Choice*, 40–41.

3. Schwartz, *The Paradox of Choice*, 40–41.

4. Tim Keller on *Carey Nieuwhof Leadership Podcast*, episode 339, May 11, 2020, https://careynieuwhof.com/episode339/.

5. Tim Keller (@timkellernyc), "So Christian identity is received, not achieved," Twitter, April 12, 2021, https://twitter.com/timkellernyc/status/1381601149854363653.

6. C. S. Lewis, *Mere Christianity* (New York: Touchstone, 1996), 190.

7. Tim Keller, "So Christian identity is received, not achieved."

Chapter 14 The Power of Agency

1. Schwartz, *The Paradox of Choice*, 113.

2. Schwartz, *Paradox of Choice*, 114.

3. Andy Crouch (@ahc), "I have to say 'no' to requests many, many times a day," Twitter, June 30, 2021, https://twitter.com/ahc/status/1410267378894655489.

Chapter 15 The One Thing We Can Control

1. Tim Keller and Kathy Keller, *God's Wisdom for Navigating Life: A Year of Daily Devotions in the Book of Proverbs* (New York: Penguin, 2017), 116.

2. Friedman, *A Failure of Nerve*, loc. 1172–73, Kindle.

3. Edwin H. Friedman, *A Failure of Nerve*, loc. 1350, Kindle.

4. "Helicopter Scene," *Jurassic World*, directed by Colin Trevorrow (2015; Universal City, CA: Universal Pictures).

About the Author

Sharon Hodde Miller leads Bright City Church with her husband, Ike. She earned her Master of Divinity from Duke Divinity School and her PhD from Trinity Evangelical Divinity School. She is the author of *Free of Me: Why Life Is Better When It's Not about You* and *Nice: Why We Love to Be Liked and How God Calls Us to More*. She speaks at churches and conferences all over the country, but her favorite city of all is Durham, North Carolina, where she and Ike are raising their three incredible kids.

Connect with Sharon!

To learn more about Sharon's
writing and speaking, visit

SharonHoddeMiller.com

f SharonHoddeMiller

🐦 SHoddeMiller

📷 SharonHMiller

Turn Your Focus from

Self to Savior

"*Free of Me* may be one of the most important truths for our times."
—ANN VOSKAMP, *New York Times* bestselling author

Free of Me

Why Life Is Better When It's NOT ABOUT YOU

SHARON HODDE MILLER

"In a culture captivated by self, this book is a must-read."

—CHRISTINE CAINE, founder of A21 and Propel Women

Experience the
Full Curriculum

Experience the
FULL CURRICULUM

 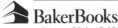